SO YOU WANT
TO BE AN
ACTOR?

For Jan

SO YOU WANT TO BE AN ACTOR?

Adrian Rendle

**Second Edition
revisions by**
Hugh Morrison

A & C Black · London

Second edition 1991
First edition 1986

A & C Black (Publishers) Limited
35 Bedford Row, London WC1R 4JH

© 1991, 1986 Adrian Rendle

ISBN 0-7136-3340-9

A CIP catalogue record for this book
is available from the British Library.

*Cover photograph by Robert Aberman of
final year student production of
Twelfth Night. Reproduced with kind
permission of Mountview Theatre
School.*

Printed in Great Britain by
Whitstable Litho Ltd., Whitstable, Kent

Contents

Acknowledgements

Thanks are due to the following for permission to reprint selected speeches from plays:

A Lily in Little India by Donald Howarth, by permission of Margaret Ramsay Ltd

The Apple Cart by George Bernard Shaw, by permission of the Society of Authors on behalf of the Bernard Shaw Estate

A Mad World, My Masters by Barry Keefe
Educating Rita by Willy Russell
Not Quite Jerusalem by Paul Kember
Sugar and Spice by Nigel Williams
By permission of Methuen, London

Teeth'n Smiles by David Hare
Not About Heroes by Stephen MacDonald
The Real Thing by Tom Stoppard
Night and Day by Tom Stoppard
Reprinted by permission of Faber and Faber Ltd

Introduction

This book is written to offer guidance and support to people who want to apply for drama training, and for those who are now just beginning their professional careers. These first few years are crucial for anyone who wants to be an actor, and I hope the book will be a useful source of information and encouragement.

If you tell someone that you want to make a career as an actor you can be sure that within two minutes the word 'precarious' will crop up. And of course acting is a very precarious career – let there be no mistake about that. The supply of actors outreaches the demand for them by tenfold. Once you choose to become an actor many people whom you thought your closest friends will tell you you're crazy, though some may react quite differently. No two people will give you the same advice. Yet it is a very personal choice you are making, and only you can assume responsibility for yourself and for realising your ambition.

There are no easy ways of getting there – no written examinations to pass, and no absolute guarantee that when you have successfully completed your training that you will automatically make your way in the profession. It's all a matter of luck plus talent. Yet there *is* a tantalising demand for new faces and new talent, and there is always the promise of excitement, glamour and the occasional rich reward. It is no accident that a popular TV series is simply called *Fame*. Fame is a spur, yes, but it is also very, very elusive.

I have frequently been asked to define this magical thing called talent, which everyone is looking out for. I believe it is best described as innate skill plus imagination – the latter being the most difficult quality to assess. It is raw imagination which often shows itself at a drama school audition, and makes the audition panel sit up and take notice. It has a lot to do with a person's courage and their conviction in what they are doing and the way they are putting it across. And in these terms, talent can be seen as basic emotional substance or susceptibility which can be developed and expanded once it is given the right emphasis and direction.

1

Where does the desire to act come from? Acting is primarily the craft of an individual, but it depends very much on creative participation with others. It is often very difficult to put into words your own reasons for wanting to act. Acting is a fugitive art: an actor's skills or performances may be memorable, but it isn't often possible to return to look at them, as with a painting, or when listening to a piece of music. True, there are films which hold up performances again and again for critical assessment, and the actor's work has been preserved in this way. Yet in the theatre the significant thing, and often the motive for acting, is that moment of contact extended by the actor on the stage to a particular audience. And it is this fleeting contact which makes up the central imaginative force and compulsion behind all acting, wherever it takes place.

The art of acting is equally hard to define, though many have tried, wittily or wisely, over the years, to capture what it is, and the aphorisms are countless. Take Ethel Barrymore: 'For an actress to be a success she must have the face of a Venus, the brains of a Minerva, the grace of Terpsichore, the memory of Macauley, the figure of Juno and the hide of a Rhinoceros.' Or Somerset Maugham, who wrote, cynically, 'By the time an actor knows how to act any sort of part he is often too old to act any but a few.'

If you ask any actor how he or she has succeeded, the response will invariably be a shrug. They will not positively know. They will know certain things about themselves and aspects of their own technique and the techniques of others. But they will take nothing for granted, because everyone knows they are only as good as their current job. It is a perverse career at the best of times.

Disappointment is the greatest enemy of the actor. Last month you might have been out of work, selling ties or waitressing. Suddenly you are asked to audition, and the prospect of an opening in the part of your life which matters most is there before you again. You live on hope.

'Oh God, I need this job', sings the girl in *Chorus Line*. Well, however much you need it, the truth is that it may be denied you. Luck is a bitch. And actors tend not to talk about their chances; they cross their fingers and look the other way, as though the opportunity hasn't really happened. They read the stars, disbelievingly yet believing – a complete paradox. And of course they devise ways of protecting themselves, against the stresses of putting themselves up for auction and the possibilty of rejection.

'I'm probably too young.'
'I'm probably too old.'
'I know they wanted a blonde.'
'Should I get rid of my beard before I go?'
'They're sure to want a name anyway.'

But could you do it?

'Oh yes, I could do it . . . but . . .'

Nobody likes being rejected. And remember that that possibility is there from the very first moment you decide you're going to become an actor, when auditioning for drama school and when you start auditioning professionally. You are saying that you are available, willing and, hopefully, talented enough for the job. And, in many ways, it's up to you, for if you don't care enough, no-one will care for you.

1 So you want to be an actor?

Everyone who wants to act professionally should try to see as much drama as they possibly can – and this means in the broadest sense, watching television, cinema, visiting the theatre and looking at the actor's work carefully and analytically. It is also important that you try and evaluate the *dramatic* experience of these different forms of presentation – this is worthwhile, because it will make you think about the different ways in which an actor can work and the various ways in which his skills are used.

Clearly, there is a difference in scale and dimension between the stage, the television screen and the cinema screen, which demand changes in direction and in acting technique. One of the things you will notice when watching the television is that close-ups are used very effectively, and so it is of vital importance that the actor has absolute control over his/her face and expression. You should also look at the ways in which the physical movements of the actor are organised to suit the restraints of the small screen.

When we turn to the theatre the question of scale is also significant. The theatre is 'larger than life', not in terms of physical scale, but because movements and speech are comparatively emphatic and intense, even when a play simulates everyday natural surroundings. Some people find this makes theatre less 'believable' – less true to their own experience and therefore less convincing than the more restrained performances seen on television and cinema.

Theatre invites you to give your full attention to what is happening on stage – the theatrical experience is a very concentrated one and you as a member of the audience are vitally connected to what is going on. As part of the audience you are as much a part of the entertainment as the performance itself, and this is something that dramatists are aware of and have always written for. Sometimes you will be directly addressed by the characters – this is something which happened a great deal in Greek and Elizabethan theatre (for example, look at the speech by Chorus in Act 4, scene 1 of *Henry V*, which draws the audience into the atmosphere before a battle enormously effectively). It is also used as a dramatic device by many contemporary playwrights.

5

The film is a very distinct dramatic medium. As you become interested in film acting it is likely that you will also become interested in film making, for the actor's work depends so much on the technical decisions of the director and editor. A film is made up of a series of shots that may be photographed over various periods of time; a 'take' that may have originally started out as three or four minutes in length may eventually be edited to a ten second shot. The film is therefore built up in pieces, a process which makes particular demands of an actor – who is also vulnerable to technical problems with cameras, lighting and editing in a way which is quite removed from the stage actor's experience. All in all, it's more difficult to evaluate an actor's work on screen, particularly as actors are usually cast in a film for their total credibility in a role and the camera work is such an intrinsic part of the final effect.

So, what can you learn from looking so closely at the actor on stage, TV and cinema? In the first place you will start to think about how an actor's work differs according to the demands of the medium. And you will become aware of technical skills – noticing economy of effect and style, seeing and hearing how an actor interprets a script, and how his thinking comes across in a performance. Of course, if an actor is doing his/her work well, you will have to work really hard to notice all these things – for the effect will be seamless.

Reading

It's very important that you read widely, both novels and playscripts, and don't just confine yourself to an exam syllabus. After all, an actor's life is spent working with words, and it will be valuable for you to have a reasonable background in the English literary and dramatic traditions.

Novels have been a rich source of material for the film industry since the talkies were introduced, and it's very interesting to see how both classic and contemporary novels require skilled adaptation of the dialogue to make sufficient dramatic impact in a film. As you read you will probably be aware of a character's potential as a role for the actor – particularly with those who have already an established place in theatrical tradition (Dickens is full of such characters).

Reading plays is an essential part of your career preparation – the more plays you read the more you will understand of the theatre's development. Academic study of drama as such is not necessarily useful for the actor, but an awareness of playwrights and their various styles *is* of practical value.

A play is primarily a piece of action and although a script contains some scenic and character description, the essential interest lies in the dialogue and the action arising from it. A play really demands to be read aloud – it needs the sound of the human voice to bring it alive. It takes imagination and a lot of practice to read a play to yourself in the same time as it would take to see it on the stage. Surprisingly, this is true of both the classical and modern play, though you might expect that the obscurities and difficulties of words and expression would prove more of a stumbling block in, say, Shakespeare or Ben Jonson.

Here is a suggested first reading list, which I've put together to provide a broadly representative selection of significant periods in the theatre's development. There is a danger in reading the classics, in that they can come to be regarded simply as literature – so always try to look at them as plays for *performance* – and, it goes without saying, try to see as much theatre as you can. It's worthwhile reading some pre-Shakespearean drama; you could read *Everyman*, a great morality play of the late Middle Ages, and *Gammer Gurton's Needle*, first performed in 1566 and thought to be the second oldest English comedy. You should try to read as much as you can of the great Elizabethan and Jacobean dramatists; Shakespeare, Marlowe and Ben Jonson, Beaumont and Fletcher, Tourneur, Webster, Middleton. Shakespeare's *A Midsummer Night's Dream* and *Hamlet* would be a good starting point – *As You Like It*, *Twelfth Night* and *Julius Caesar* you may already be familiar with, as they are often set for O level courses. Marlowe's *Dr Faustus* and Ben Jonson's *Volpone* and *The Alchemist* are frequently revived.

You might well enjoy Beaumont and Fletcher's rumbustious *The Knight of the Burning Pestle* – *The Maid's Tragedy* is a good choice, too.

The Jacobean dramatists created a world of passion and violence, vividly theatrical. Two of the best plays to read from this period are Tourneur's *The Revenger's Tragedy*, and Webster's *The White Devil*.

Theatres were closed during the Cromwellian period, but with the restoration of the monarchy in 1660 came Court comedy and the beginning of the 'comedy of manners' which has, in one way or another, been popular right up to the present day. William Congreve's *Love for Love* and *The Way of the World* are highly decorated in language, and sharp in wit; to compare with these, you could look at William Wycherley's more 'basic' comedy, *The Country Wife*.

Perhaps the most 'modern' of the Restoration writers is George Farquhar; period artifice is not so obtrusive in his plays, the best known of which are *The Recruiting Officer* and *The Beaux Stratagem*. It would also be a good idea to read something by the French dramatist, Molière, their great contemporary, who satirises the hypocrisies of cultivated society; I recommend *Tartuffe* about a religious imposter and *La Malade Imaginaire*, a satire on the medical profession. Sheridan and Goldsmith continued to write comedies of manners during the eighteenth century, with their famous plays *The Rivals* and *She Stoops to Conquer*, and this tradition finds its most successful twentieth-century exponents in Noel Coward and Somerset Maugham; *Private Lives* and *The Circle* are frequently revived by present day repertory companies. Have a look at these.

The nineteenth century was, by and large, an unexciting time for theatre writing, until the end of the century when Oscar Wilde and George Bernard Shaw make their entry. Wilde's *The Importance of Being Earnest* is a *must* and of the large Shavian canon I suggest you read *St Joan* and *The Doctor's Dilemma* or *Major Barbara* to get a clear idea of his style and the kind of demands he makes of actors verbally.

The most vital explosion of British theatre writing since the Second World War came with the foundation of the English Stage Company at the Royal Court Theatre in London, under the direction of George Devine: the first season mounted there included John Osborne's *Look Back in Anger*. Arnold Wesker's famous trilogy of plays *Chicken Soup with Barley*, *Roots* and *I'm Talking About Jerusalem* was also performed at the Royal Court.

You should be aware of this period and I recommend reading all four plays and also *The Theatre of George Devine* by Irving Wardle.

Harold Pinter occupies a unique place in contemporary theatre as a distinctive stylist, and I suggest you read some of his early short plays like *The Room* and *The Dumb Waiter* before going on to his major plays like *The Birthday Party* and *The Caretaker*. Two of the most outstanding of recent playwrights are David Hare and Tom Stoppard, and I have included extracts from their work in the audition piece selections, p 31. I recommend that you read Hare's trilogy *The History Plays*, which include *Knuckle*, *Licking Hitler* and *Plenty* – and perhaps his earlier play *Teeth n' Smiles*. Stoppard's most popular play is probably still *Rosencrantz and Guildenstern are Dead*, and he has had notable success with *Jumpers*, *Travesties*, and, more recently, *The Real Thing*.

Two other contemporary writers whose work was first performed by the English Stage Company are Nigel Williams, author of *Sugar n' Spice* and Paul Kember, author of *Not Quite Jerusalem* (which has recently been filmed). It's worth reading these two plays. And you should also read Steven Berkoff, a high stylist and writer of abrasive poetic theatre, who stands quite alone. Look at *East*, *Greek* and *Decadence*.

I haven't yet mentioned the development of the Theatre of the Absurd, which has been a strong force in European drama since Alfred Jarry's *Ubu Rio* was first performed in 1896. Read *Ubu*, and you can see the connections with Samuel Beckett's *Waiting for Godot*, and Ionesco's *The Chairs* and *The Bald Prima Donna*. Martin Esslin's book *The Theatre of the Absurd* is a very valuable background on this subject. Of the British playwrights, Pinter is often thought to be on the edges of 'absurdism' and you could also read N.F. Simpson's *One Way Pendulum* and *Cresta Run*.

All of these recommendations, however, are only to give you a first taste of the scope of theatrical writing. You should read as much as you can of European and American drama, both historical and contemporary, for by doing so you will certainly set yourself up well for both drama school training and your subsequent acting career.

2 *Approach to drama training*

One of the questions you may be asking yourself is 'Can I be taught to act?' This is something everyone wonders when starting out, even if they are not intending to make a living out of acting. The answer is, of course, no. No-one can actually *teach* anyone to act. That has something to do with the indefinable thing called talent. You either have it or you do not – talent is certainly not something which can be taught. But talent can be developed and trained and provide a sound basis for you to give of the best there is inside you. So at this moment it's as well to look at your present experience and see how you can help yourself to extend it, before applying to audition at a drama school.

First training opportunities

Your local amateur society is always a good beginning. Being nervous and taking risks are two of the main things you will have to face as an aspiring actor, and that first time you read a play with a group of strangers, rather than in a classroom or among friends is when you confront your first hurdle. But you may not actually *learn* much, simply because the main object of the group will not be to help you but to get on and do the play, relying on the skills available and hoping that the audience will give adequate support.

So what else can you do? In recent years the amateur actor has had more opportunity for classes in theatre work, including voice and movement training as well as performance and directing skills. These facilities differ in all parts of the world, but in Britain the evening class is probably the most accessible form of training. London is obviously where most of the opportunities abound. Notable here are the courses offered during both day and evening by the City Literary Institute.

Classes at the 'City Lit', as it is affectionately known, are handled by a highly competent team of tutors, many of whom teach at the drama schools too. There are classes in movement, dance, acting and improvisation, as well as more specialist areas like mime, clowning, and playwriting. The classes are on certain days of the

11

week only, but enrolment is not expensive given that a term is structured over the usual academic year. The term can be approximately twelve to thirteen weeks long, and advanced classes will in all probability do a production over that time which will be mounted and produced in the Institute's own theatre. Such an exercise might even spread over two or three terms.

What should you do if you don't live in London, and find that it is financially difficult to pay for such courses? The best way to find out about what is available to you more locally is to contact your County Drama Adviser and also the Regional Arts Association for your area, who will have details about part-time training for young actors (see Appendix A). Amateur theatre flourishes almost everywhere, and when you're beginning it cannot be stressed too strongly that it is desirable to obtain some actual stage experience before jumping into the big pool of drama school, or even summer school. Once again, the Regional Arts Association will know the leading amateur companies in your area, and this should certainly help you in looking for the kind of group to which you are best suited.

The British Theatre Association, mentioned in the first edition of this book, has for decades offered professional and all-embracing training courses for actors, directors, and young people. It is currently, in 1990, fighting for its life. Due to lack of governmental or any other official support this unique and valuable organisation has had to suspend its training activities temporarily, whilst trying to secure for itself a sound and permanent financial basis for the future. It is hoped that courses on a limited basis may restart in the Autumn of 1990. Meanwhile, the BTA is still the custodian of the finest theatre library in Europe. It would be a tragic loss to theatre if such an important organisation were to go to the wall. It's been the cradle and help of many actors, directors and playwrights.

The summer school

The summer schools or workshops offered by the drama schools last approximately five weeks, and give a clear idea of what full-time drama training involves. And one of the main advantages of these very compressed and arduous courses is that they give students approaching drama school entry an opportunity of seeing what will be required of them should they gain a place at drama school.

The workshops run daily from 9.30 a.m. to 5.00 p.m. (Monday to Friday), giving a taste of the kind of stamina that will ultimately be required over a much longer period. (At drama school the full-time course will frequently require the student to work until 9 p.m. and later when productions are being mounted.) Because summer schools generate enormous interest overseas, there is nearly always a strong emphasis on the classical theatre, usually on Shakespeare, and there will quite probably be classes on classical texts and mini-production exercises arising from these. You may find yourself doing quite a bit of 'line learning'.

The daily schedule can be something like this:

9 a.m.	Movement/dance
10 a.m.	Voice/Speech class
11 a.m.	Text analysis, or a class in the direction of text where students try out their own interpretations
Noon	Improvisation
1 p.m.	Lunch
2 p.m.	Make-up class
3 p.m.	Rehearsal of course project
5.30 p.m.	End of classes for the day

The five weeks is structured to provide a fairly comprehensive picture of actor training though even so it can only provide an outline of classes at drama school. There is not much time for academic work, though some courses include lectures on theatre history. Some of the courses include a limited number of visits to the theatre, and discussion of these productions will be included in the overall schedule. But acting and all that it means is very much a doing thing, so the emphasis is always on practical work.

Anyone can participate in summer schools, as no auditions are required, only completion of an application form. But often students attending *do* have previous experience, either in the amateur theatre, or in university or school productions. On the whole there is no real age limit, and the level of experience can be very mixed. Classes are led by experienced staff, usually by staff at the drama school where the course is held, and at the end of the five weeks groups will present mini-production projects to each other, on which they will be assessed, and they will usually be given a certificate for having attended the course. In some cases students wishing to take an open audition for the full-time course may do so without paying the usual audition fee.

The cost of training at a summer school over a five-week period will vary with the different establishments, but the overall fee is likely to be around £700 (1990 prices), for all students, whether from Britain or overseas. For details about applying to summer schools, see Appendix C on p 134.

3 *Going to drama school*

Vocational training for the actor as we know it has only existed in England for the last eighty years. The starting point was the formation by Sir Herbert Tree of a training school at His Majesty's Theatre, London, in 1904. The school later moved to Gower St, was granted a royal patent, and eventually became the Royal Academy of Dramatic Art.

Eighty years doesn't seem a very long time when you consider the art of acting has been prospering in Europe over the last four hundred or so years, quite apart from the great traditions of ancient Greek drama. But it is certainly true that in the last sixty years the various schools and academies of acting have had a significant effect on the climate of acting. It's significant, too, that while Herbert Tree was laying the foundations of drama training in England, the famous partnership of Stanislavsky and Danchenko in Russia was beginning, and saw the first developments towards the establishment of the Moscow Arts Theatre. Stanislavsky's ideas on acting became central to modern drama training, and many of the most interesting and powerful concepts in actor training developed from his work.

Choosing your course

Most people applying to drama school will be seeking to enrol on the full-time diploma course, which usually runs over a three-year period. The average age of entry for the diploma course is between 18 and 20, though some schools accept entrants as young as 17, others students up to 30: age between these limits is not likely to be a problem provided the candidate shows talent, flexibility and motivation. Some schools offer a two-year course for students who have more experience, particularly those from overseas. Two-year course students may be a little older, and have already studied drama at university level.

A limited number of schools offer post-graduate courses which are scheduled over one year. LAMDA (London Academy of Music and Drama) runs a one-year course for overseas students only, which although not set up as a post-graduate course may include a

15

number of students with extensive university theatre experience as well as some professional experience. Drama Studio London also runs a one-year course for post-graduate students or in some cases students with other professional skills or theatrical experience.

Obviously, sorting out the courses which are on offer can best be done by writing for the prospectus but with any application the question that will be of overriding importance is how you are going to finance your training.

Payment of fees and grants

Fees set by each drama school do differ slightly, though they can be considered basically similar. In general, it's wise to think of each term's tuition fees as costing from £1300 to £1600 (prices current in 1989/90). Expect a general rise in fees of some 7-9% for the academic year starting September 1990. For an eight-term diploma course the total cost will be around £11–12000. These fees are quite distinct from the money you will need for living, travelling, buying books, etc., which will probably account for a further £3500 to £5000 (these figures are based on 1989/90 standards). Three-year and two-year diploma students should bear these figure in mind so they have some idea of what is going to be involved when they make an application for a further education grant to their local authority.

Application for a grant should be made at the same time as the application for an audition in order that you can be sure of your position should you be fortunate enough to be offered a place. It is true that some local authorities will not say whether you are eligible or not until a place has been put on offer to you, but it's still very much worth your while to find out all you can from your local education authority.

Discretionary grants for further education have suffered in the climate of recent economic cuts and local government spending allowances can affect the number and level of grants awarded. Generally, a local authority will aim to cover the full cost of fees and a living allowance, although this can be subject to your personal circumstances and will vary depending on whether you will live with your parents during term time, or in rented accommodation.

It is possible that your local authority may ask you to audition for them after you have been offered a place. This seems an odd way of going about things, but the advising panels do carry a professional adviser so that talent is not merely being judged by local civil servants. The object of this rather clumsy piece of administration is to place some check on the expenditure of local money on the arts – and also to provide a further checkpoint on students who have already received educational grants for other careers. Having worked on interview panels with the now defunct ILEA I can say that the object has not been to block the drama school selection so much as to see that the grant is well justified.

Scholarships are an entirely different matter. Some schools do provide for students to be granted a scholarship towards the cost of tuition, but there are not many endowments of this kind. RADA offers two to three scholarships per year for UK students, Webber Douglas offers two, RSAMD offer a small number of scholarships and Guildford School of Acting offers one to an acting student, for fees only. LAMDA have a small number of awards, some of which can give financial assistance. Two scholarships are available for American students at RADA, which provide the total fee, or, according to parental income, part of it.

Drama schools in Britain

There are seventeen drama schools in Britain which constitute the 'Conference of Drama Schools' and most of these have courses which have been accredited by the National Council for Drama Training. This means they have been inspected by a team of professional experts and the standard of their work has been approved. Drama training is under constant review through the accreditation system, so that standards are maintained and new developments assessed, and schools which may not be in the accredited list today may well be there soon.

Any potential student will naturally wish to see what is offered by the different drama schools and a concise summary of the aims and policies of the seventeen main schools can be found in Appendix B on p 119. There are, of course, many schools other than those listed in the appendix, and also a great many private coaches, all of whom may be found in the publication *Contacts*, a trade book everyone interested in joining the profession should obtain from the office of *The Spotlight*, 42–43 Cranbourn St,

London WC2H 7AP. In the 1984 edition a further one hundred and thirty-four addresses were listed, which includes ballet schools, mime tuition courses, and others.

There are still those who prefer to take their chances in the profession without any formal training. This used to be a lot easier to do than it is now: for one thing, working in the profession means that you have to belong to the actors' union, Equity. Yet students who have completed expensive training face the same difficulties as an untrained actor in qualifying for an Equity card. This question is discussed later in the book, but it is still relevant to the potential drama student. Becoming an actor has to be thought of in realistic terms right from the beginning and all possible problems do need to be faced.

The post-graduate course

The post-graduate course is not offered by all drama schools, and places are therefore limited. As far as grants are concerned, students who apply for a place are almost certain to have used at least three years' worth of their local authority grant entitlement while studying at university or polytechnic, and may only be eligible for a further one-year entitlement if they have been accepted at a drama school. And it has been said that local authorities are not always very sympathetic to acting as a choice of career and sometimes obtaining a grant may be more difficult if a student has evidently changed his or her career tack.

The case of a physics teacher who wanted to become an actor is interesting in showing the kind of problems which accompany a late entry into drama school. The local authority to which he applied refused to provide the necessary grant, and the person was sadly compelled to turn down a place on a one-year post-graduate course which had already been offered to him. The grounds were that he had used up his grant entitlement in qualifying to be a teacher.

The three or four terms offered to post-graduate students condense the technical work of a three-year course; on the whole there is greater emphasis on training the voice, movement, acting technique, fencing and dance, etc. since students will presumably have developed a fair amount of performing skill through their university drama departments or societies. This means that there is usually only one 'show-case' production at the end of the year for agent and production managements to see. The one-year course is only to lay down the foundations of good technical training – and it is widely recognised that the course simply pushes the student into the profession with enough practical experience to find his or her feet. There is an optional second year which students can apply for which 'joins up' with the two-year diploma course. Students don't automatically proceed to this – it depends on the talent of the individual concerned, and of course it means that an extra year's funds have to be found.

There is really no way of knowing how long it takes to develop an actor who has already gained a lot from work in university. University acting can be very good and technically aware, or it can be immensely self-indulgent and over-academic, full of theory and sparse on craft. That is why the post-graduate course exists – to shape intellect and enthusiasm and provide practical and professional skills.

The overseas student

All major drama schools audition in the USA, and offer places to students who can show talent and raise the money to accept a place. This is one field of higher education where in some cases the fees from the overseas student are no higher than they are for British nationals. In all cases students taking a course (which is usually either a two-year diploma course or a one-year course) are expected to return to their country on completion of training. Students can also apply from any part of the world, and audition in the UK, but need to remember that a high standard of fluency in the English language will be expected. There will always be problems when working with an English vernacular text using cockney or other dialects, but students from overseas have to expect to take this in their stride (and usually do).

Undoubtedly one of the best ways the overseas student has of seeing what is required in British theatre training is to apply for one of the summer schools offered by the drama schools, and find out what it's all about before committing him- or herself to a long and expensive stay. It's important that a student is prepared to understand and work with the prevalent theatrical traditions in UK schools.

And with so much theatre training available in the United States, New Zealand, Australia and Canada, it is interesting to ask why

British theatre training is thought to be so beneficial. I can only put it down to the strong classical emphasis which prevails in the courses offered in the UK, although many of the university drama courses in the USA do stage Shakespeare and the European classical authors. America has had many unsuccessful attempts to form a national repertory theatre, performing the classics of the English language, and one wonders whether it will ever be possible to get this going effectively. It's often thought that previous attempts have failed because there aren't enough well-trained classical actors in the USA to make such a repertory company feasible, but this is increasingly not the case: American drama students are eager to train in the UK, and the percentage of successful auditions held is relatively high. In Great Britain the ear becomes accustomed to the native British voice handling the classical text, but this really should not hinder American actors; they need not become totally 'accentless' in order to play classical verse. Instead they need to find out the rhythms of speech which make the music of the verse work in dramatic form. Many American students working in British drama schools find the answer to this question by using what is called 'standard American', and this approach is being used now in training on both sides of the Atlantic.

4   *The drama school audition*

By now you will have made a definite decision to become an actor – no matter what the problems or obstacles. The next step is to prepare for the audition at a drama school and find the right kind of textual material which will allow you to show the best of yourself.

On obtaining a prospectus and asking for an application form, you will find that every drama school will require an audition fee, and this can vary between £15 and £25. If you can afford to, it's generally best to spread your auditions around the drama schools so that you are seen more than once.

When auditioning for most schools you will be asked to present at least two contrasting speeches and possibly give some idea of your attitude to improvisation and, perhaps, to singing. It's usual to make a choice from the classical and modern repertoire. Some schools will stipulate a number of Shakespearean speeches from which you may select, but in the main the choice of work is left entirely to you.

Your choice of material

A lot will depend on your current theatre experience and whether you have done much acting, but finding the right kind of character to work in an audition is going to mean some careful thinking and planning. Always think what the chosen piece is doing for *you* – after all, the audition is about you, the naked ape, as well as that inner spark of inspiration you may have. *Your* bones, *your* eyes, *your* hair, *your* teeth are all going to be scrutinised by a panel of judges who are looking for your all-round potential, not just an impressive academic display. Acting is very much a physical business.

Remember that there may be some twelve to eighteen places at any one of the drama schools, and the number of auditions may number up to fifteen hundred for the leading schools. Don't be daunted by that, but recognise that like everything else in the acting business, it is highly competitive. No drama school panel is looking for the ultimate in audition technique but candidates should possess a noticeable degree of competence and self-awareness.

Not all auditions have just two speeches, classical and modern. You may well be asked to sing something unaccompanied, or do a short improvisation and you may well be asked to perform one of the speeches in a different way. In some schools you will be asked to participate with other students in basic class work over a weekend (as happens at the Bristol Old Vic drama school) and in some you may find yourself being judged partly by senior students of the school who will be sitting with the faculty panel (which is something that happens at Drama Centre). The point of preparation is to be well tuned and at the same time flexible to new interpretations and ideas. Rigidity of approach is something to be avoided at all costs – there is no point in being able to do a 'party piece' one way and be unable to take in new direction on the same material.

Everyone on the audition panel is prepared to be on your side and supportive. They are not looking for you to fail – every audition panel wants you to be good. That's why there are contrasting pieces; not everyone is going to be marvellous with the classics (Rex Harrison once avowed that he was 'no good at Tudor verse speaking'). But you are expected to be competent with such material even if you feel this is not what you would eventually choose to work with. The classical text is for the panel to see your present abilities, your imaginative range and your capacity as a thinking actor. And while you are not expected to be perfect (who is, ever?) you are expected to have something to offer.

The classical audition

Shakespeare is the most widely known and read of the classical playwrights and it is for this reason that a piece from one of his plays is nearly always obligatory at a drama school audition. This is not simply to force people into speaking blank verse, but to see how a person responds to the essential humanity of a character – for Shakespeare, of all the classical writers, is probably the most human, whose work is blessed with both grandeur and the common touch.

The plays are full of characters that soliloquise – that is, speak solo without other characters around them, thinking aloud about their aims, their problems, their ambitions, loves and hatreds.

These soliloquies occupy a unique area of dramatic speech (although the solo aria is something modern dramatists are now using more frequently).

There are a host of audition pieces to be derived from the soliloquies and monologues, many of which are well tried favourites, and almost any selection will be reasonably well known. But when you are looking for a suitable speech you can't really reject anything familiar solely because you think it might bore the panel. It's true that extracts such as Phoebe's 'Think not that I love him . . . ' from *As You Like It* (Act 3, Scene 5) or Viola's 'I left no ring with her . . . ' from *Twelfth Night* (Act 2, Scene 2) may be all too well known to a panel, but I cannot agree with an adjudication policy that would ban these pieces from the audition. The selection is right if it truly works for the competing student, and it is the quality and force of the imagination that will carry off the performance of the piece. The most important thing is your firm knowledge that the selection is within your present range. It's not much use arriving somewhere at ten in the morning clutching the collected works under your arm and wishing you had a wig and been born thirty years earlier in order to play Lear – or for that matter the Duke of Gloucester. Major roles for older women are not so common in Shakespeare, but I think it is better not to choose a character such as Queen Katherine from *Henry VIII*, who needs a richness of seniority to convey the dramatic interest. If you do want to portray an older figure, it would be preferable to try Hermione in *The Winter's Tale* – she is a more fantastical character, without the added complications of historical authenticity, and so allows for greater flexibility of characterisation. Her trial scene (Act 3, Scene 2) which begins

> Since what I am to say must be but that
> Which contradicts my accusation . .

is a familiar but effective choice.

In Shakespeare there are many young men to choose from. Romeo is a good choice, and there are many speeches to look over and consider, but think also about the not so familiar young lover Troilus; Bassanio, Lorenzo and Graziano, from the *Merchant of Venice* all make good choices too. And of course there is Petruchio, lively in humour and making a confidante of his listeners. All of them have speeches that are rich in passion, character and intensity, which can sustain the actor in solo flight. The point is that they are all vital young men with love on their minds, full of colourful words to express their feelings, and all are within the range of the eighteen to twenty-five year old student actor.

And then there are the tougher types: Edmund from *King Lear*, a romantic macho figure with a wide eye for fame and fortune. You might also think about that other bastard son, Philip, in *King John*, a merry, pranking, politically astute fellow, with a wry, salty style. He has a famous eulogy on status:

> A foot of honour better than I was
> But many a foot of land the worse . . .
>
> (Act 1, Scene 1)

Much in the same vein is *Henry V* who has several well known 'set' speeches, full of fireworks, as well as the difficult and testing soliloquy on the responsibility of leadership that begins 'Upon the King . . . ' (Act 4, Scene 2). This is a major meditative speech brooding on the loneliness of the man caught between action and passivity – thinking aloud in much the same way as Hamlet does in his many renowned arias on the soul and the theme of revenge.

And remember there is no need to be afraid of Hamlet. He is, after all, an actor's part and perfectly accessible – he prefers, too, to be acted rather than to be read. Years of scholarship and so many contentious performances mean that the character is now regarded as 'difficult', when it can in fact benefit from the freshness and vitality of the natural actor, who will quickly find the comic qualities of the man as well as his serious side.

Ophelia is often ignored for audition material simply because she doesn't seem to have much in the way of a sustained speech until she goes mad. Yet her earlier speech, where she describes Hamlet's condition and behaviour, has great tenderness and awareness:

> He took me by the wrist, and held me hard,
> Then goes he to the length of all his arm,
> And, with his other hand thus o'er his brow,
> He falls to such perusal of my face
> As he would draw it . . .
>
> (Act 2, Scene 1)

The speech is short but very telling and can be effective in a solo audition, even though the actual scene does involve other characters.

The question of selection is very personal; after all, what makes you choose the character that you are going to do? There must be some affinity between you and the man or woman on the printed page – something that you recognise not because you are 'just like that' but because you feel that you can interpret the situation with those words.

Let us look at *Romeo and Juliet*. One thing you can be sure of is that the panel will know the words of these characters very well (they will probably be able to prompt you at any given moment should you 'dry') but each and every time the lines are spoken by a new voice they are different in their texture, humour, drama and music. Bernard Shaw once described *Romeo and Juliet* as 'the impetuous march of music', and if ever there was a play of rich language, this is it. The music of the words is there to be used – but not at the expense of the sense and emotional content. Although every moment of the lovers' experience is drenched in imagery, there is still a fine feeling of reality about the characters which gives them bone and muscle. Yet it is not the reality of a naturalistic drama, such as we would find in, say, Ibsen or Chekhov. We cannot explain the motivations of Romeo in terms of today's values, but we can bring a contemporary handling to the words that will make the imagery blaze afresh each time it is spoken.

You will find the speeches scattered like jewels throughout the text, but it is perhaps as well to keep to the simpler ones for your audition piece – those where Romeo and Juliet are directly enthralled by love and the declaration of love to another person. These are better than the poison-taking and tomb scenes. In any case, keep your chosen speech short and contained, for it is better to end when those auditioning would have you continue. Brevity truly is the soul of wit.

Reading around for background to Shakespeare is valuable, and you can't do better than begin with the Harley Granville Barker's *Prefaces to Shakespeare*, which analyse the plays from both a scholarly and dramatic angle, without being ponderously academic. John Barton's *Playing Shakespeare* is a fine follow-up. Barton does investigate the actor's work in a more contemporary way and the book is based on the TV series of the same name.

The modern audition

Selections from the modern theatre may include characters that have been created over the last sixty years, from Noel Coward to

Steven Berkoff. Which is a very big range. Interestingly, though, most of the audition selections are chosen from work of the last twenty years; most young students will go for contemporary work. Therefore the pieces that have been put together in the following pages as possible audition selections are from writers who have gained, or are now gaining, a major place in contemporary theatre.

In my suggested audition pieces, I have not included any of the well known speeches from such modern classics as *Look Back in Anger*, by John Osborne, or *Roots*, by Arnold Wesker although these plays are revived frequently in many theatres. Neither have I suggested anything from Noel Coward, Somerset Maugham or Terence Rattigan, even though their plays are continually being performed. The technique required in presenting characters from these plays is usually more delicate than can be achieved in a first audition, whereas the work of Tom Stoppard, David Hare and Barry Keefe (for example) is more easily grasped by the young actor. Finding characters for yourself will, I think, depend a good deal on your personal taste in theatre at the time you are auditioning. And your choice of audition piece is often largely decided by the contrast it provides with the classical selection you have made. The question of accent is important too – you need to be confident of the accent with which you are working, and it is always advisable to present an accent you are familiar with or at least can work with comfortably.

The first piece of advice that's necessary is that you shouldn't just try to be fashionable by choosing juicy speeches that catch your eye without knowing the whole play and having a working idea of how to perform the speech. And don't let your search for material lead you to choose the obscure for obscurity's sake, so you feel you will be sure to stun the panel with a piece that has no good professional background. Similarly, extracts from Agatha Christie or general run of the mill commercial theatre very rarely have enough substance on which you can work. A piece to be presented should have something more than a surface narrative quality in the characterisation. Writers such as C.P. Taylor, David Halliwell, Peter Nicols, Caryl Churchill and Louise Page have a great deal to offer. But there are many more, of course, and listing playwrights is useful only insofar as it presents a few guidelines, primarily to help you look in the right places.

There are also many opportunities for audition pieces in the American repertoire. Arthur's Miller's plays such as *All My Sons* and *Death of a Salesman* are now regarded as virtual classics, and so are Tennessee William's *Cat on a Hot Tin Roof*, *The Glass Menagerie* and *A Streetcar Named Desire*. American theatre is well known and well regarded here, and to choose a piece from any of those just mentioned is thoroughly viable. Sam Shepard and Edward Albee are also good choices, and there are interesting selections to be made from the play of the book *One Flew Over the Cuckoo's Nest*, by Dale Wasserman.

One of the most electric and abrasive of contemporary dramatists is Steven Berkoff, who uses big classical rhythms in his work, which calls for the sustaining power of 'total' theatre, rather than naturalistic treatment. Berkoff demands high technical skill, but is wide open to raw interpretations, and as such offers a lot to the auditioning student. If you try him I suggest you select from *Greek* or *East* rather than, say, the more recent *Decadence*: the latter play contains enormous speeches, usually much longer than you will need, and is fearfully difficult material to cut.

Berkoff makes particular demands on the actor. There are no character notes of any kind in the text, which is written as a complex rhyming scheme that looks like prose at first glance. He sets up long, colourful and emotional speeches that are in turn both funny, beautiful and violent, and his work cannot be compared with anything that has preceded him. Finding a style in these parts without having seen a production of the play can be a problem, but as with absurd drama, there is a lot of room for personal interpretation.

Few auditions seem to be chosen from the works of Samuel Beckett – *Waiting for Godot* and *Endgame* are the only two which seem to offer possibilities. On the other hand, Harold Pinter's characters Mick and Aston from *The Caretaker* are familiar, and both of them are still young and exciting enough to make good choices.

Remember that anything which excites and interests you is a possibility and the greater the contrast with your first classical choice, the better you will enable the panel to see your present range.

Coaching and presentation

You will now perhaps be wondering whether or not you should be coached for your audition. Coaching can be a great help – but it can also get in the way, for slavishly following a pedantic teacher can produce very strange results, with the candidate ending up trying to sound like someone he or she isn't. Your natural ability is the thing that should emerge, and if you have been well coached the coaching won't show. If you have been badly coached it will show everywhere. So it's another of those difficult personal decisions. Choose your coach with care; be sure that they know what they are doing for the theatre and actor of today. There are plenty of good coaches about just as there are a multitude of nice misguided types who seek to portray themselves through other people over and over again. You are the actor on show at your audition – no-one is interested in auditioning your coach.

Valuable coaching can often come from drama school tutors who can give a fair assessment of the possibilities you may have prior to auditioning. A list of such tutors is contained in *Contacts* (address is given on p 17). It can be well worth the additional expense of some private tuition for the audition and gaining one to one advice on your material.

Your own presentation is another thing you need to be aware of. Clothes are important – you should wear something which enhances your own self esteem and creates the right kind of impression. This is sometimes regarded as old fashioned thinking, unfortunately, and it's a shame, for although clothes don't actually make you perform better a good comfortable appearance does give the panel a chance to see how you see yourself and how your body uses clothes.

When presenting a classical and a modern piece women may use a practice skirt for one selection which can be used over jeans, or another skirt. Men may wish to use a jacket for one piece and only a sweater for the other. And props; what do you do about them at your audition? Well, anything that can be carried and produced without a lot of fuss is permissable – pipes, cigarettes, mirrors, handbags, fans, matches, etc. But the less elaborate you can be the better. Try to think of the essentials, as any good coach will tell you. For example, if you are embarking on Julia in *Two Gentlemen of Verona* and her Proteus letter, it is as well to have a sheet of paper that you can tear up to make the scene start with a dramatic focus and give the lines some action.

Learning thoroughly the piece which you are going to do is important. Auditions *are* nerve-wracking for everyone who does them (and for that matter, for everyone who watches them) but being sure of your text is the least you can do. Should that unthinkable thing happen, and you forget your lines, don't despair. A sympathetic panel may well ask you to start again. But there is no trick to the business of learning lines, as you will find out as you go on – although learning lines for an audition is different from memorising a part in a play for production, because then you will be operating with other actors around you. On the whole, acting in isolation is a peculiar feature of the audition system, which is why the pieces you choose in either the classic or modern text need to be reasonably well contained and lend themselves to being performed as a one man show.

If you have done any class work before attempting the drama school audition, most of the teachers will at some point in their sessions have talked about 'relaxation'. A lot has to do with how you breathe and how you react physically to moments of tension. You will be tense at the audition because a lot is at stake, but if you trust to your own natural resources, the degree of panic can be reduced. I would suggest that if you are sure of your pieces, don't read them over and over again on the way to the audition – once will be quite enough.

Nerves afflict everyone in some way, and without them acting would be the poorer. The dead calm actor is, on the whole, dead boring. Stage nerves are unlike anything else in the whole world, and many good actors will confess to them right through their careers. Stage fright is something else – but it is usually self-induced and can be overcome, finally, with much rehearsal practice.

When dealing with nerves, the most important single thing is to have a centre of concentration. Concentration has nothing to do with gritting your teeth and braving it out; it's the secret of being more and more relaxed and aware of everything that is going on at the same time. You will not only be sure of the text, but, more than this, of the character you are portraying. With well written characters the words fit and flow so that the actor can ride with ease, and the thoughts, no matter how disjointed, have a natural quality that is at once 'actable'.

No-one can hope to have a command of all these things at a first audition. But they are guidelines to what acting is basically about.

5 *Audition selections*

Here is a selection of speeches for both men and women that may be recommended for auditions at drama schools. It can't be stressed enough that you should know the entire play from which you select your audition piece; not only that, but have thought carefully about the characters and their inter-relationship.

The classical text

Romeo and Juliet by William Shakespeare.

Mercutio is in high spirits, teasing Romeo about his love as they prepare to go to the Capulet masked ball. He speaks to both Romeo and others around him, about dreams and dreamers.

MERCUTIO   O then I see Queen Mab hath been with you.
She is the fairies' midwife, and she comes
In shape no bigger than an agate stone
On the forefinger of an alderman,
Drawn with a team of little atomi
Over men's noses as they lie asleep.
Her chariot is an empty hazelnut
Made by the joiner squirrel or old grub,
Time out o' mind the fairies' coachmakers;
Her waggon-spokes made of long spinners' legs,
The cover of the wings of grasshoppers,
Her traces of the smallest spider web,
Her collars of the moonshine's watery beams,
Her whip of cricket's bone, the lash of film,
Her waggoner a small grey-coated gnat,
Not half so big as a round little worm
Prick'd from the lazy finger of a maid;
And in this state she gallops night by night
Through lovers' brains, and then they dream of love;
O'er courtiers' knees, that dream on curtsies straight;
O'er lawyers' fingers who straight dream on fees;
O'er ladies' lips, who straight on kisses dream,
Which oft the angry Mab with blisters plagues
Because their breaths with sweetmeats tainted are.

Sometime she gallops o'er a courtier's nose
And then dreams he of smelling out a suit;
And sometime comes she with a tithe-pig's tail,
Tickling a parson's nose as a lies asleep;
Then dreams he of another benefice.
Sometime she driveth o'er a soldier's neck
And then dreams he of cutting foreign throats,
Of breaches, ambuscados, Spanish blades,
Of healths five fathom deep; and then anon
Drums in his ear, at which he starts and wakes,
And being thus frighted swears a prayer or two
And sleeps again. This is that very Mab

Act 1, Scene 4

Comment

This is a very well known piece, which needs vivacity and spontaneity in presentation; Mercutio is enjoying himself, weaving his way through a fantastical set of images. The problem lies in sustaining the speech, for Mercutio is a hearty and boisterous character, seemingly at odds with the mischief and delicacy of this speech. Would such a man talk of fairies like this? Yet he obviously loves taunting Romeo about the 'sickness' of love.

King John by William Shakespeare

Philip the Bastard, half brother to Robert Faulconbridge, and son of King Richard the First, discovers himself in a position of authority when King John knights him and dubs him Sir Richard Plantagenet. Left to his own reflections, he reveals himself to be a bright, keen opportunist.

BASTARD   Brother, adieu: good fortune come to thee!
For thou wast got i'the way of honesty.

[*Exeunt all but the bastard*]

A foot of honour better than I was,
But many a many foot of land the worse.
Well, now can I make any Joan a lady.
'Good den, Sir Richard!' – 'God-a-mercy, fellow!' –
And if his name be George, I'll call him Peter;
For new-made honour doth forget men's names:
'Tis too respective and too sociable
For your conversion. Now your traveller,

He and his toothpick at my worship's mess,
And when my knightly stomach is suffic'd,
Why then I suck my teeth, and catechize
My picked man of countries: 'My dear sir,' –
Thus, leaning on mine elbow, I begin,
'I shall beseech you,' – that is Question now;
And then comes Answer like an Absey book:
'O sir,' says Answer, 'at your best command;
At your emloyment; at your service, sir:'
'No, sir,' says Question, 'I, sweet sir, at yours;'
And so, ere Answer knows what Question would,
Saving in dialogue of compliment,
And talking of the Alps and Apennines,
The Pyrenean and the river Po,
It draws toward supper in conclusion so.
But this is worshipful society,
And fits the mounting spirit like myself;
For he is but a bastard to the time
That doth not smack of observation;
And so am I, whether I smoke or no.
And not alone in habit and device,
Exterior form, outward accoutrement,
But from the inward motion to deliver
Sweet, sweet, sweet poison for the age's tooth:
Which, though I will not practise to deceive,
Yet, to avoid deceit, I mean to learn;
For it shall strew the footsteps of my rising.
But who comes in such haste in riding-robes?
What woman-post is this! Hath she no husband
That will take pains to blow a horn before her?
O me! 'tis my mother. How now, good lady?
What brings you here to court so hastily?

Act 1, Scene 1

Comment

The character talks freely about himself, and what he hopes to gain from his new rank. The jokes and the conversations end abruptly with 'But this is worshipful society' and at that point he shows his real toughness and ambition. The piece needs to be taken at a good pace and in high spirits.

The Merchant of Venice by William Shakespeare

Lorenzo with his Jessica await the return of Portia, remaining out in the still night rather than returning to the house.

LORENZO   Sweet soul let's in, and there expect their coming.
And yet no matter: why should we go in?
My friend Stephano, signify (I pray you)
Within the house, your mistress is at hand,
And bring your music forth into the air.

                                        [*Exit Stephano*]

How sweet the moonlight sleeps upon this bank!
Here will we sit, and let the sounds of music
Creep in our ears – soft stillness and the night
Become the touches of sweet harmony:
Sit Jessica, – look how the floor of heaven
Is thick inlaid with patens of bright gold,
There's not the smallest orb which thou behold'st
But in his motion like an angel sings,
Still quiring to the young-ey'd cherubins;
Such harmony is in immortal souls,
But whilst this muddy vesture of decay
Doth grossly close it in, we cannot hear it: . . .
For do but note a wild and wanton herd
Or race of youthful and unhandled colts
Fetching mad bounds, bellowing and neighing loud,
Which is the hot condition of their blood, –
If they but hear perchance a trumpet sound,
Or any air of music touch their ears,
You shall perceive them make a mutual stand,
Their savage eyes turn'd to a modest gaze,
By the sweet power of music: therefore the poet
Did feign that Orpheus drew trees, stones and floods;
Since naught so stockish, hard and full of rage,
But music for the time doth change his nature, –
The man that hath no music in himself,
Nor is not moved with concord of sweet sounds,
Is fit for treasons, stratagems, and spoils;
The motions of his spirit are dull as night,
And his affections dark as Erebus:
Let no such man be trusted: – mark the music.

                                        Act 5, Scene 1

Comment
This extract is made up of two consecutive speeches to Jessica; either

speech can be played for an audition, but if you have the time to do them both together the extract works well. Remember that this is an intimate scene with Jessica, and you should identify her clearly throughout. Allow the freshness of the thoughts to dominate, letting one idea lead into another.

Love's Labours Lost by William Shakespeare

Berowne confesses to his love for Rosaline, with a good deal of witty, self mockery.

BEROWNE   O! and I forsooth in love!
I, that have been love's whip;
A very beadle to a humorous sigh;
A critic, nay, a night-watch constable,
A domineering pedant o'er the boy,
Than whom no mortal so magnificent!
This wimpled, whining, purblind, wayward boy,
This senior-junior, giant-dwarf, dan Cupid;
Regent of love rhymes, lord of folded arms,
The anointed sovereign of sighs and groans,
Liege of all loiterers and malcontents,
Dread prince of plackets, king of codpieces,
Sole imperator and great general
Of trotting paritors: O my little heart!
And I to be a corporal of his field,
And wear his colours like a tumbler's hoop!
What! I love! I sue! I seek a wife!
A woman that is like a German clock,
Still a-repairing, ever out of frame,
And never going aright, being a watch,
But being watch'd that it may still go right!
Nay to be perjur'd, which is worst of all;
And among three, to love the worst of all;
A whitely wanton with a velvet brow,
With two pitch-balls stuck in her face for eyes;
Ay and by heaven, one that will do the deed
Though Argus were her eunuch and her guard:
And I to sigh for her! to watch for her!
To pray for her! Go to; it is a plague
That Cupid will impose for my neglect
Of his almighty dreadful little might.

> Well, I will love, write, sigh, pray, sue, and groan:
> Some men must love my lady, and some Joan.
>
> Act 3, Scene 1

Comment

Berowne almost seems to revel in his own discomfiture here, in his desperate last stand for freedom – he clearly enjoys the sensation of falling in love, even though he presents the experience as a disaster! Invite the audience to listen to your dilemma, and keep the pace quick, for there is nothing solemn about Berowne.

Titus Andronicus by William Shakespeare

Aaron is a Moorish soldier of fortune, who with his mistress, Tamora, has been captured by the Romans in their war against the Goths.

AARON

Now climbeth Tamora Olympus' top,
Safe out of fortune's shot, and sits aloft,
Secure of thunder's crack or lightning flash,
Advanc'd above pale envy's threat'ning reach.
As when the golden sun salutes the morn,
And, having gilt the ocean with his beams,
Gallops the Zodiac in his glistering coach,
And overlooks the highest-peering hills;
So Tamora.
Upon her wit doth earthly honour wait,
And virtue stoops and trembles at her frown.
Then, Aaron, arm thy heart, and fit thy thoughts,
To mount aloft with thy imperial mistress,
And mount her pitch whom thou in triumph long
Hast prisoner held, fett'red in amorous chains,
And faster bound to Aaron's charming eyes
Than is Prometheus bound to Caucasus.
Away with slavish weeds and servile thoughts!
I will be bright, and shine in pearl and gold,
To wait upon this new-made empress.
To wait, said I? to wanton with this queen,
This goddess, this Semiramis, this nymph,
This siren that will charm Rome's Saturnine,
And see his shipwreck and his commonweal's.
Holla! what storm is this?

Comment
This is one of the great roles for a black actor (not that black actors in these days are not eligible to play practically any character in Shakespeare, with the exception of Desdemona!). Aaron, lover of Tamora, has been brought to Rome a captive, then freed. He is relishing his future. He is a witty, ruthless adventurer: a strange and exotic outsider in Rome, and a villain on the grand scale. To scan, Semiramis should be pronounced SeMIRamis not SEMiramis.

Love's Labours Lost by William Shakespeare

Rosaline chides Berowne, and taxes him with certain conditions he must fulfil if he is to gain her hand (the Princess and her ladies have responded to the death of the King of France by postponing any further romance for one year).

ROSALINE   Oft have I heard of you, my Lord Berowne,
                 Before I saw you, and the world's large tongue
                 Proclaims you for a man replete with mocks;
                 Full of comparisons and wounding flouts,
                 Which you on all estates will execute
                 That lie within the mercy of your wit:
                 To weed this wormwood from your fruitful brain,
                 And there withal to win me, if you please,
                 Without the which I am not to be won,
                 You shall this twelve month term from day to day,
                 Visit the speechless sick, and still converse
                 With groaning wretches; and your task shall be,
                 With all the fierce endeavour of your wit
                 To enforce the pained impotent to smile.

BEROWNE   To move wild laughter in the throat of death?
                 It cannot be; it is impossible:
                 Mirth cannot move a soul in agony.

ROSALINE   Why, that's the way to choke a gibing spirit,
                 Whose influence is begot of that loose grace
                 Which shallow laughing hearers give to fools.
                 A jest's prosperity lies in the ear
                 Of him that hears it, never in the tongue
                 Of him that makes it: then, if sickly ears,

> Deaf'd with the clamours of their own dear groans,
> Will hear your idle scorns, continue then,
> And I will have you and that fault withal;
> But if they will not, throw away that spirit,
> And I shall find you empty of that fault,
> Right joyful of your reformation.
>
> Act 5, Scene 2

Comment

It's important to pick the right vocal note for Rosaline, as her wit and sexuality need to be put across here. Rosaline is very much a match for Berowne; this is her last challenge to him, at a moment in the play when death has blown all comedy away. Her challenge is, in itself, almost cruelly witty, and Rosaline must be seen to relish the situation, rather than becoming priggish. Essentially, what she wants is for Berowne to discover what is serious in life, and to stop fooling all the time.

Measure for Measure by William Shakespeare

Isabella has visited Angelo to plead for her brother's life. Angelo offers her a bargain: if she will sleep with him her brother shall live. This speech is her shocked reaction to Angelo's 'proposal'.

ISABELLA To whom should I complain? Did I tell this,
Who would believe me? O perilous mouths,
That bear in them one and the self-same tongue
Either of condemnation or approof,
Bidding the law make curtsey to their will,
Hooking both right and wrong to th' appetite,
To follow as it draws! I'll to my brother.
Though he hath fall'n by prompture of the blood,
Yet hath he in him such a mind of honour,
That had he twenty heads to tender down
On twenty bloody blocks, he'd yield them up
Before his sister should her body stoop
To such abhorr'd pollution.
Then, Isabel live chaste, and brother, die:
More than our brother is our chastity.
I'll tell him yet of Angelo's request,
And fit his mind to death, for his soul's rest.

Act 2, Scene 4

Comment

Isabella can very easily come across as a prig. Her virtue is so important to her that she can more easily contemplate her brother sacrificing his life to save her virginity than that she might sacrifice herself for him. Isabella perceives clearly the game Angelo is playing: here she is angry and frustrated – don't try and make her too 'nice' a character.

Two Gentlemen of Verona by William Shakespeare

Julia with a letter in her hand, speaks first to Lucetta. Some lines previous to the main speech have been incorporated here.

JULIA   This babble shall not henceforth trouble me.
           Here is a coil with protestation.

                          [*She tears the letter.*]
           Go, get you gone; and let the papers lie.
           You would be fing'ring them, to anger me.

                            [*Lucetta leaves*]
           Nay, would I were so anger'd with the same!
           O hateful hands, to tear such loving words;
           Injurious wasps, to feed on such sweet honey,
           And kill the bees that yield it, with your stings!
           I'll kiss each several paper, for amends.
           Look, here is writ 'kind Julia': – unkind Julia!
           As in revenge of thy ingratitude,
           I throw thy name against the bruising stones,
           Trampling contemptuously on thy disdain.
           And here is writ 'love-wounded Proteus'.
           Poor wounded name: my bosom, as a bed,
           Shall lodge thee till thy wound be thoroughly heal'd;
           And thus I search it with a sovereign kiss.
           But twice, or thrice, was 'Proteus' written down:
           Be calm, good wind, blow not a word away,
           Till I have found each letter, in the letter,
           Except mine own name: that some whirlwind bear
           Unto a ragged, fearful, hanging rock,
           And throw it thence into the raging sea.
           Lo, here in one line is his name twice writ:
           'Poor forlorn Proteus', 'passionate Proteus'.
           'To the sweet Julia': that I'll tear away.
           And yet I will not, sith so prettily
           He couples it to his complaining names.

Thus will I fold them, one upon another:
Now kiss, embrace, contend, do what you will.

Act 1, Scene 2

Comment
The essential qualities of this character are her impulsiveness and
her youthful alertness. How far does she commit herself to Proteus,
and does she really criticise herself? Think out your actions so that
they enhance the text.

As You Like It by William Shakespeare

Rosalind, disguised as a young man (Ganymede) speaks to Phoebe,
who clearly considers her to be an attractive male. Rosalind
comments shrewdly upon her own sex in her admonishment of
Phoebe.

ROSALIND   And why I pray you? Who might be your mother,
That you insult, exult, and all at once,
Over the wretched? What though you have no beauty –
As by my faith I see no more in you
Than without candle may go dark to bed –
Must you be therefore proud and pitiless?
Why what means this? Why do you look on me?
I see no more in you than in the ordinary
Of Nature's sale-work. 'Od's my little life,
I think she means to tangle my eyes too!
No faith proud mistress, hope not after it.
'Tis not your inky brows, your black silk hair,
Your bugle eyeballs, nor your cheek of cream,
That can entame my spirits to your worship.
You foolish shepherd, wherefore do you follow her
Like foggy South puffing with wind and rain?
You are a thousand times a properer man
Than she a woman. 'Tis such fools as you
That makes the world full of ill-favour'd children.
'Tis not her glass but you that flatters her,
And out of you she sees herself more proper
Than any of her lineaments can show her.
But mistress, know yourself, down on your knees,
And thank heaven, fasting, for a good man's love;
For I must tell you friendly in your ear,

Sell when you can, you are not for all markets.
Cry the man mercy, love him, take his offer;
Foul is most foul, being foul to be scoffer.
So take her to thee shepherd. Fare you well.

Act 3, Scene 5

Comment

A very well known audition piece, but nonetheless valid for all that.
Don't, on any account, go for a heavy-handed male impersonation
here – Rosalind is an intelligent woman, with a sense of humour,
and she is enjoying herself responding to Phoebe's rather obvious
games.

A Midsummer Night's Dream by William Sheakespeare

TITANIA   These are the forgeries of jealousy:
And never, since the middle summer's spring,
Met we on hill, in dale, forest or mead,
By paved fountain, or by rushy brook,
Or in the beached margent of the sea,
To dance our ringlets to the whistling wind,
But with thy brawls thou hast disturb'd our sport.
Therefore the winds, piping to us in vain,
As in revenge have suck'd up from the sea
Contagious fogs; which, falling in the land,
Hath every pelting river made so proud
That they have overborne their continents.
The ox hath therefore stretch'd his yoke in vain.
The ploughman lost his sweat, and the green corn
Hath rotted ere his youth attain'd a beard;
The fold stands empty in the drowned field,
And crows are fatted with the murrion flock;
The nine-men's-morris is fill'd up with mud,
And the quaint mazes in the wanton green
For lack of tread are undistinguishable.
The human mortals want their winter cheer:
No night is now with hymn or carol blest.
Therefore the moon, the governess of floods,
Pale in her anger, washes all the air,
That rheumatic diseases do abound.
And thorough this distemperature we see
The seasons alter: hoary-headed frosts

Fall in the fresh lap of the crimson rose;
And on old Hiems' thin and icy crown,
An odorous chaplet of sweet summer buds
Is, as in mockery, set; the spring, the summer,
The childing autumn, angry winter, change
Their wonted liveries; and the mazed world,
By their increase, now knows not which is which.
And this same progeny of evils comes
From our debate, from our dissension;
We are their parents and original.

Act 2, Scene 1

Comment
The piece includes a great deal of descriptive colour; only try it if you feel you can bring something of your own imagination to it, and be prepared to risk some indulgence. Keep Titania tough, springy and challenging: this speech is an accusation, and the expression of her grievance against Oberon.

The Beaux' Stratagem by George Farquhar

Mrs Sullen is a young gentlewoman, living in the country much against her will, and chafing against marriage to a drunken brute.

MRS SULLEN   Country Pleasures! Racks and Torments! dost think, Child, that my Limbs were made for leaping of Ditches, and clambring over Stiles; or that my Parents wisely foreseeing my future Happiness in Country-pleasures, had early instructed me in the rural Accomplishments of drinking fat Ale, playing at Whisk, and smoking Tobacco with my Husband; or of spreading of Plaisters, brewing of Diet-drinks, and stilling Rosemary-Water with the good old Gentlewoman, my Mother-in-Law . . . . Not that I disapprove rural Pleasures, as the Poets have painted them; in their Landscape every Phillis has her Coridon, every murmuring Stream, and every flowry Mead gives fresh Alarms to Love. – Besides, you'll find, that their Couples were never marry'd: – But yonder I see my Coridon, and a sweet Swain it is Heaven knows; – Come, Dorinda, don't be angry, he's my Husband, and your Brother; and between us both is he not a sad Brute?

O Sister, Sister! if ever you marry, beware of a sullen, silent Sot, one that's always musing, but never thinks: – There's some Diversion in a talking Blockhead: and since a Woman must wear Chains, I wou'd have the Pleasure of hearing 'em rattle a little. – Now you shall see, but take this by the way – He came home this Morning at his usual Hour of Four, waken'd me out of a sweet Dream of something else, by tumbling over the Tea-table, which he broke all to pieces, after his Man and he had rowl'd about the Room like sick Passengers in a Storm, he comes flounce into Bed, dead as a Salmon into a Fishmonger's Basket; his Feet cold as Ice, his Breath hot as a Furnace, and his hands and Face as greasy as his Flanel Night-cap. – O Matrimony! He tosses up the Clothes with a barbarous swing over his Shoulders, disorders the whole Economy of my Bed, leaves me half naked, and my whole Night's Comfort is the tuneable Serenade of that wakeful Nightingale, his Nose. – O the Pleasure of counting melancholly Clock by a snoring Husband! – But now, Sister, you shall see how handsomely, being a well-bred Man, he will beg my Pardon.

Comment

Mrs Sullen is anything but sullen. She describes the horrors of matrimony with vivacious comic indignation, dazzling wit and choice of expression, and with breathtaking eloquence. She is young and pretty, and filters her fury through irresistible humour. She is **not** bitter, cynical, languid, or camp. I've left the original spelling and orthography to give a feel of the vigour of the language. It must be one of the funniest speeches ever written for an actress, and needs a bubbly, light touch. Not for the novice, but still worth attempting.

The Relapse or *Virtue in Danger* by John Vanbrugh

Lord Foppington arrives at the London house of Loveless and Amanda. Foppington recently 'bought' his peerage; he was formerly known as 'Sir Novelty Fashion', and he speaks with gusto and effrontery, his speech deliberately affected, turning his 'o's to 'a's.

FOPPINGTON   Far to mind the inside of a book, is to entertain one's self
with the products of another man's brain. Naw I think a
man of quality and breeding may be much better diverted
with the natural sprauts of his own. But to say the truth,
madam, let a man love reading never so well, when once
he comes to know this tawn, he finds so many better ways
of passing the four-and-twenty hours, that 'twere ten
thousand pities he should consume his time in that. Far
example, madam, my life; my life, madam is a perpetual
stream of pleasure, that glides through such a variety of
entertainments, I believe the wisest of our ancestors never
had the least conception of any of 'em.
   I rise, madam, about ten a-clock. I don't rise sooner,
because 'tis the worst thing in the world for the complex-
ion; nat that I pretend to be a beau; but a man must
endeavour to look wholesome, lest he make so nauseous
a figure in the side-bax, the ladies should be compelled to
turn their eyes upon the play. So at ten a-clack, I say, I rise.
Naw, if I find 'tis a good day, I resalve to take a turn in the
Park, and see the fine women; so huddle on my clothes,
and get dressed by one. If it be nasty weather, I take a turn
in the chocolate-hause: where, as you walk, madam, you
have the prettiest prospect in the world; you have looking-
glasses all round you. – But I'm afraid I tire the company.

Act 2, Scene 1

Comment
A rich restoration character, not recommended unless there is some
reasonable experience working in the style. Foppington is the
King of Fops; hard and witty, not soft and camp; relish the tartness
of his delivery, his enjoyment of the spoken word.

The modern text

Not Quite Jerusalem by Paul Kember

Mike, a Cambridge undergraduate who is working on a kibbutz is
talking to the Jewish girl Gila and explaining why he left university
to end up in Israel. He finds it difficult to describe his feelings and
says at first 'I just walked out.' Gila presses him to explain his
reasons to her.

MIKE   I don't know. I was just sitting on the grass one day, down by the river. [*Pause*] Everyone else was lying around and I just thought: 'That's it, I've had enough'. And I just walked away leaving everything – clothes, money, records, books . . .

And I walked. I just kept walking. Walking and walking in the pissing rain. I just walked. Nothing momentous. No dead birds fell from the trees. No portents. I just walked, all the way along Trumpington Road. [*Pause*] I got as far as Grantchester and I thought, fuck it, yes, why not? Do it. The heart of England trip. Get in touch with the true essence of England, what it is to be English. Let the village atmosphere seep into your pores. See if you can make contact with it, this magical thing called Englishness. I wanted to see if I could experience it. The place was deserted. I kept walking, past the old mill, right up around the bend to where the council property starts, and I thought, oh, shit, council houses. I'm never going to find the spirit of true Englishness there. So I headed back to the village. Looked at all the usual things; the cottages, the rectory and so on and, eventually ended up in the churchyard; the one where Rupert Brooke is buried. And there's the poem presumed to be about the clock stopping. And it's all so wonderful and idyllic. And I was scouting around vaguely aware that, in fact, I'd actually located it. The English ideal. That this essence of Englishness was actually there in my possession . . . And suddenly I caught sight of this . . . prat sailing down the Cam back towards Cambridge in a punt, with a girl doing all the work, while he reclined at the exact angle, trying to play a chord and strum a tune . . . There was this idiot, sailing along desperately trying to simulate an atmosphere of . . . Christ knows 'Some vague recollection of tranquillity from his grandfather's scrapbook.' It was all there. The spires in the background, the river, this typical English village – and this prat – this arch tit – sailing through the stillness of centuries – absolutely fucking clueless. [*Pause*] I walked out of the village, got to the main road, turned right instead of left and here I am. How do you put that in a letter? [*Pause*] Are you any wiser?

Comment

No particular accent is asked for, but Mike is not the conventional public school type who has gone to Cambridge. He speaks with really quite a small vocabulary which suggests he is unused to expressing himself eloquently. Part of the time he may almost be unaware that he is speaking to another person – after all Gila doesn't understand English very well and it is unlikely that she would fully understand the references to Rupert Brooke and the poem 'The Old Vicarage, Grantchester'. (Suggest that you read that poem as a background.)

Not Quite Jerusalem by Paul Kember

Carrie is in her mid to late twenties and comes from Birmingham. She talks incessantly and seems over-enthusiastic about nearly every aspect of life – prattling on without caring much about the kind of responses she gets from other human beings around. In this speech (comprising in fact two consecutive speeches) she talks to Mike about herself and impressions of the kibbutz life.

CARRIE   Oh, yes. I must say, I had certain ambitions for higher education myself, but when you receive the call, as they say, those cherished dreams just have to go by the board. Not that I would have attempted to scale the academic heights of an Oxford or a Cambridge, of course, but they do do some very stimulating courses at the Birmingham Polytechnic. Mind you I've taken the precaution of leaving all my nursing manuals at home. If you're going to take a break it may as well be a clean one.
Incidentally, have you been to the kibbutz library yet? Tuesdays seven to nine p.m. They've got some very interesting works. Unfortunately most of them are in Hebrew. But there's quite a stack of paperbacks left behind by other volunteers. It's pretty lightweight, most of it and what isn't lightweight is salacious, so I wouldn't think you'd find much to stimulate you there, but you could try. I was in there last night trying to get some ideas for Volunteers Day. Not that I managed. You know, of course, we had our second meeting last night? Needless to say, nobody turned up. I sat for half an hour outside the dining room like a pickle in a jam factory. Oh, don't worry, I'm not getting at you. You were probably busy working, I appreciate that. It's the others I'm worried about.

Comments

This is a straight comedy speech (though the character does not find herself funny). She is a busybody who likes talking and has cultivated her own style. Her Birmingham background is hinted at and if you can manage a Birmingham accent it might be useful, but it is not essential in finding the character.

Teeth'n Smiles by David Hare

Arthur is a twenty-six year old song writer in the world of rock music, *c.* 1975, (the date the play was first performed at the Royal Court Theatre).

ARTHUR   Where I first met Maggie. She was singing in the *Red Lion*. She was sixteen, seventeen, a folk singer. Let us go a pickin' nuts, fol de ray, to Glastonbury Fair, a tiddle dum ay. I had to carry her over the wall, can you imagine, to get her to my rooms. They build walls here to stop undergraduates making love. Well, we got caught, of course, by this very Mr Snead coming in satirical German manner, even shining a torch, an English suburban stormführer. He hauled me up to my tutor, who said, do you intend to marry the girl? I said, not entirely. He said, as this is a first offence you will not be sent down, instead, I fine you ten pounds for having a girl on the premises. I said what you mean like a brothel charge? I was furious, I was out of my mind.

   [He takes another cigarette]
Thanks. And everyone told me: don't waste your energy. Because that's what they want. They invent a few rules that don't mean anything so that you can ruin your health trying to change them. Then overnight they redraft them because they didn't really matter in the first place. One day it's a revolution to say fuck on bus. Next day it's the only way to get a ticket. That's how the system works. An obstacle course. Unimportant. Well, perhaps.

Comment

This is reflective speech; the character seems rootless and so there is no definite accent or background indicated. We gather that he comes from the university where they are now playing the concert.

After taking the cigarette (an important prop in this speech) Arthur changes tack. He seems to be talking in a series of jumpy thoughts. For this reason the speed of the speech may be slower than it looks, the cigarette smoking being used to punctuate it.

Teeth'n Smiles by David Hare

Maggie, in between numbers at a rock concert, talks to Laura about the young student who has just made love to her.

MAGGIE   He was in a bit of a state, I couldn't believe it. I think he must have juiced himself up. He said your thighs are so beautiful, your thighs are so beautiful, well, Laura, you seen my thighs. I said please let's not . . . I'd rather you just . . . He said your body is like a book in which men may read strange things, a foreign country in which they may travel with delight. Your cheeks like damask, the soft white loveliness of your breasts, leading to the firm dark mountain peaks of your, Laura, now I'm dreading which part of my body he will choose next on which to turn the great white beam of his fucking sincerity. Between your legs the silver comets spiral through the night, I lose myself, he says . . . he says . . . how beautiful you are Maggie and how beautiful life ought to be with you.

[*Pause. She cries*]

Then eventually . . . I say please, faking. He says yes of course, he stops talking. We wait. For thirty minutes. For thirty minutes it is like trying to push a marshmallow into a coinbox.

[*Pause*]

Then he manages. In his way. Afterwards he says it's his fault. I say no mine, perhaps the choice of location . . . he says it can't be your fault, you have made love to the most brilliant and beautiful men of your generation, you have slept with the great. I say there are no great, there is no beautiful, there is only the thin filth of getting old, the thin layer of filth that gets to cover everything. So. Off he goes. Ta ta.

Comment

Maggie is a young, burnt-out pop singer. The piece requires delicacy, to express the real awfulness she senses in her life. The phrasing needs particular care.

The Real Thing by Tom Stoppard

Debbie, the teenage daughter of the writer Henry, talks with her father about his work and about her own life. In this extract three speeches have been linked together.

DEBBIE   What, *House of Cards*? Well, it wasn't about anything, except did she have it off or didn't she? What a crisis. Infidelity among the architect class. Again.

Most people think *not* having it off is *fidelity*. They think all relationships hinge in the middle. Sex or no sex. What a fantastic range of possibilites. Like an on/off switch. Did she or didn't she. By Henry Ibsen. Why would you want to make it such a crisis?

It's what comes of making such a mystery of it. When I was twelve I was obsessed. Everything was sex. Latin was sex. The dictionary fell open at *meretrix*, a harlot. You could feel the mystery coming off the word like musk. *Meretrix*! This was none of your *mensa-a-table*, this was a flash from the forbidden planet, and it was everywhere. History was sex, French was sex, art was sex, the Bible, poetry, penfriends, games, music, everything was sex except biology which was obviously sex but obviously not *really* sex, not the one which was secret and ecstatic and wicked and a sacrament and all the things it was supposed to be at one and the same time – I got that in the boiler room and it turned out to be biology after all. That's what free love is free of – propaganda.

Act 2, Scene 7

Comment

A seventeen year old, bright and intelligent enough to put herself on an equal footing with her father. She does have affection for him but is not over-impressed with his success as a writer and she speaks directly from her own experience rather than any vicarious sensations. Be careful not to create anyone with a phoney Chelsea 'Sloane' accent or anything outrageous. She speaks good standard English without any affectation.

The Real Thing by Tom Stoppard

Henry, a successful playwright, is being pushed by his wife to re-write or adapt a play by a raw young man called Brodie, who is in prison. Henry has no wish to do this and chooses to explain to Annie why he finds Brodie's work clumsy and ill-constructed.

[*He holds up a cricket bat.*]

HENRY   Shut up and listen. This thing here, which looks like a wooden club, is actually several pieces of particular wood cunningly put together in a certain way so that the whole thing is sprung, like a dance floor. It's for hitting cricket balls with. If you get it right, the cricket ball will travel two hundred yards in four seconds, and all you've done is give it a knock like knocking the top off a bottle of stout, and it makes a noise like a trout taking a fly . . . [*He clucks his tongue to make the noise.*] What we're trying to do is to write cricket bats, so that when we throw up an idea and give it a little knock, it might . . . travel . . . [*He clucks his tongue again and picks up the script.*] Now, what we've got here is a lump of wood roughly the same shape trying to be a cricket bat, and if you hit a ball with it, the ball will travel about ten feet and you will drop the bat and dance about shouting 'Ouch!' with your hands stuck into your armpits. [*Indicating the cricket bat.*] This isn't better because someone says it's better, or because there's a conspiracy by the MCC to keep cudgels out of Lords. It's better because it's better. You don't believe me, so I suggest you go out to bat with this and see how you get on. 'You're a strange boy, Billy, how old are you?' 'Twenty, but I've lived more than you'll ever live.' Ooh, ouch!
[*He drops the script and hops about with hands in his armpits, going 'Ouch!'*]

Act 2, Scene 2

Comment

A mature man, Henry speaks with style and wit about the art of playwriting to his wife (who is prepared to listen!). The speech is rich in comic sensitivity. Taking a cricket bat to the audition isn't a bad idea although you can get the same effect with an umbrella. In fact the props of the speech are important and not too difficult to use to help your presentation.

Night and Day by Tom Stoppard

The play is set in a imaginary African Republic, Kambawe. In this scene the country's President, Mageeba, talks with an Australian journalist. The president is finely educated and is capable of talking like a professor and behaving like a despot. This piece includes several speeches edited together.

MAGEEBA   At the time of independence the *Daily Citizen* was undoubtedly free. It was free to select the news it thought fit to print, to make much of it, or little, and free to make room for more girls wearing less and less underwear. You may smile, but does freedom of the press mean freedom to choose its own standards? . . .

That was the question. Easy enough to shut the paper down, as I would have been obliged to do had it not been *burned* down during the state of emergency which followed independence. But what to put in its place? The English millionaire folded his singed tents and stole away the insurance money, which didn't belong to him since I had nationalized the paper well before the fire was out. Never mind – the field was open. I did not believe a newspaper should be part of the apparatus of the state; we are not a totalitarian society. But neither could I afford a return to the whims of private enterprise. I had the immense and delicate task of restoring confidence in Kambawe. I could afford the naked women but not the naked scepticism, the carping and sniping and the public washing of dirty linen which represents freedom to an English editor. What then? A democratic committee of journalists? – a thorn bush for the editor to hide in. No, no – freedom with responsibility, that was the elusive formula we pondered all those years ago at the LSE. And that is what I found. From the ashes there arose, by public subscription, a new *Daily Citizen*, responsible and relatively free. [*He leans towards Wagner*] Do you know what I mean by a relatively free press, Mr Wagner? . . . I mean a free press which is edited by one of my relatives.

[*He throws back his head and laughs.*]
Act 2

Comment

For a black actor this speech gives a major opportunity to convey power and style. Mageeba makes no concessions to the white political world yet he understands a great deal about it. Ask yourself about the current African political scene and read round it to find interesting parallels, since Mageeba represents a mixture of the kind of African leadership to be found.

A Lily in Little India by Donald Howarth

Alvin Hanker is in his room. He has just broken one of his records deliberately and is on his knees picking up the pieces as he talks to himself.

ALVIN   You're silenced forever if your groove's not joined. I'm sorry I broke you in sacrifice. [*He rises and puts the pieces into the drawer of the chest of drawers*] Never mind. I'll get you another one again. [*He mimics his mother's voice*] 'If only you'd read for once or play cards. Find yourself a hobby like other people, go to the pictures, the night school, the dancing, the football, the . . . ' Night school. If I went to night school I'd be a student. Alvin student. There are too many. Students all trying. Besides, there's only one for the top of the class. I might look well with a hobby. If you have a private sideline, that's it. No-one expects you to present the result. [*He sits in the chair*] You can do it when you come home from work and you're all right at week-ends. I could dance. I could be taught. [*He mimics a young woman's voice*] 'Bert Shutt's Palais's no good for dancing with Alvin Hanker.' [*He rises and takes an imaginary partner*] A dance floor's for partners. [*He dances*] Four legs behave as two on the ballroom boards. [*He steps on his partner's toes*] Never mind dancing. [*He sits*] Too many dance. Too many legs on ballroom floors, crowding each other out on to the pavements. Dancing's overcrowded like the pavements. All going to the pictures. I like the pictures. Sitting in the pictures – getting dark and warm and watching with the music all the time playing from nowhere. Film stars are real and all first class with big faces – and they're good at it. I get on well at the films. It would be sitting at the pictures if I could have the money to do it full time. I could borrow. But there's the travelling to get to the one the night after and seeing a different one every middle of the week. I couldn't afford the fares into town as well as a reasonable seat for sitting in. Playing at cards isn't for one, except Patience. But I cheat so that's out. I could read. It's quiet. I could read a lot. Seven books a week. Library books. Long books – full of quiet reading far from Mrs Raistrick's ears. Books with photographs beside the print, beautiful, like film stars, but quiet. Slender, thin-backed books with titles, books on buildings, books on ships, on bridges, books on end, books on wardrobes never dusted, books on gardening books. Flower books on flowers.

Act 1

Comment

This character has a northern accent and the fact is important to the handling of the piece. He is on his own and definitely talking aloud to himself in the privacy of his room. There is no need to over-play the slightly pathetic quality but seek out the eagerness of his search for something to do. His imitations of other voices calls for a good sense of mimicry, and should bring the dreariness of his life into focus. Perhaps you could have two pieces of broken gramophone record with you as a prop to start the extract.

Not about Heroes by Stephen Macdonald

This is a play for two characters, Siegfried Sassoon and Wilfred Owen, the World War One poets, and it would obviously be a good thing to read some of their poetry as a background to performing this piece. Sassoon survived the war and died in 1967. Owen, seven years younger, was killed one week before the war ended. The play is an imaginative reconstruction of their friendship.

SASSOON   By the 8th June, I was back in the front line. Our mission was to take back from the Boche those few miles of battered ground that we'd bought with half a million lives in those Battles of the Somme, two years before. I found myself in the same place where I'd been wounded in Easter, 1917. Hundreds of thousands of lives had bought nothing, had proved nothing. I wonder . . . what was *I* trying to prove? Just that I was not a *sheep*, waiting to be slaughtered, at their command. And nor would I lead my company to be slaughtered, at their command. Another Protest, I suppose. Even more ineffectual than the first. All I did was to out on a raid – unofficially. And when the sun came up in no-man's-land, it was hot. A beautiful summer morning. I took off my tin hat to feel the sun on my face. And I didn't hear the bullet leaving the rifle. One moment I was revelling in the astonishment of being alive, and the next – I was lying flat on my face, with what felt like a very large hole in the right side of my skull . . . They carried me back to England in the middle of July. My war seemed to be over. I couldn't understand why I'd not been killed when there were so many others who . . . It took me a long time to accept the fact that now I should not be killed – that I should be one of the survivors.

After all that I was going to live on . . . alone . . . to write the 'Memoirs' . . . to listen to Mozart in Salzburg.

OWEN   . . . In a village near Amiens, I found a shop where you can still get tea, and enough cakes to make a schoolboy sick for a week. I'll remember when I go up the line . . . That will be any hour now.

I feel confident because I know I came out to help: directly, by leading them as well as an officer can; indirectly, by watching their sufferings so that I may plead for them as well as I can. I have done the first . . .

Very dear Siegfried. I have been in action some days. Our experience passed the limits of abhorrence: I lost all my earthly faculties and fought like an angel. You'll guess what happened when I say that I am now commanding the Company – and in the line I had a seraphic boy-lance-corporal as my sergeant-major. I have mentioned my excellent batman, Jones. In the first wave of the attack he was shot in the head and thrown on top of me. He lay there dead, his blood soaking my shoulder for half an hour. It's still there, crimson, on my tunic.

I can't say I suffered anything – having let my brain grow dull. My nerves, then, are in perfect order. My senses are charred. I shall feel again as soon as I dare, but now I must not. I don't take the cigarette out of my mouth when I write 'Deceased' across their letters . . . Siegried, I don't know what you'll think, but I've been recommended for the MC – and I've recommended every single NCO who was with me. I'm glad of it – for the confidence it will give me at home.

I think it's all over for a long time. Moreover, the war is nearing an end. Do you know what you will do? What are you doing now? Can you tell me?

(In this extract several pieces of Owen's dialogue have been put together.)

Comment

Sassoon
Sassoon was a public school man (read his book *Memoirs of a Fox-hunting Man*) and his slightly cold style is only a front for his real feelings. It is probably best to take this piece seated, to suggest a character looking back reflectively at the events recalled.

Owen
Owen was from Shropshire, from a less smart background than Sassoon. Don't try to play the speech poetically. There are many shifting thoughts to be considered in this extract, and there is colour too; you need to convey the spurts of energy vocally.

The Apple Cart by George Bernard Shaw

The play is a fable, of an England ruled over by King Magnus. Orinthia is his mistress and this speech is taken from an amusing scene between Orinthia and Magnus. Orinthia replies to Magnus's words 'It must be magnificent to have the consciousness of a goddess without ever doing anything to justify it.'

ORINTHIA   Give me a goddess's work to do; and I will do it. I will even stoop to a queen's work if you will share the throne with me. But do not pretend that people become great by doing great things. They do great things because they are great, if the great things come along. But they are great just the same when the great things do not come along. If I never did anything but sit in this room and powder my face and tell you what a clever fool you are, I should still be heavens high above the millions of common women who do their domestic duty, and sacrifice themselves, and run Trade departments and all the rest of the vulgarities. Has all the tedious public work you have done made you any the better? I have seen before and after your boasted strokes of policy; and you were the same man, and would have been the same man to me and to yourself if you had never done them. Thank God my self-consciousness is something nobler than vulgar conceit in having done something. It is what I am, not what I do, that you must worship in me.

Comment

There is more to this speech, but this seems a good place to stop for a short and effective audition. Orinthia is an expansive, richly styled character, based on the exotic personality of actress Mrs Patrick Campbell. The voice needs to be rich and varied, flirtatious and worldly wise.

A Mad World, My Masters by Barry Keefe

This is a modern version of the Elizabethan 'City' comedy, a panorama of town life, teeming with villains, mugs, lechers and madmen. The atmosphere is rich and steamy, Superintendant Sayers tries with little success to keep order.

SUPT. SAYERS   Hello Hello . . . hardly what you'd call grief with a large G. I smell a con. I smell it as surely as I smell a knocked off car, a crooked log book. One previous owner? Who's that – Julius Caesar? My wit numbs them to speechlessness. Then I pounce with devastating questions to expose their guilt. Like Magnus Magnusson I am. An intrepid interrogator. Twenty five years in the service, 43 murder cases. All that, and I still can't get a mortgage. No home, no mortgage, that's me. I've seen the places I want. Lovely little mock Tudor semis in the wog-free suburbs. But these mortgage companies, they don't want to know . . . Nor the councils. They say no, 'cause I've got a police house. Look, mate, I've got nothing against these Indians, Chinese, Pakistanis, Blacks you name 'em I've got nothing against them – apart from them being here. But what I want to know is this – how come a Pakistani hot off the banana boat can get a mortgage when a decent cop with 25 years service in the force cannot? Look mate, what this country needs is someone to look up to. Someone to stop all this weak kneed nancy pancying pussy footing soft balls hard luck Jim have another large scotch. I went to Northampton to try and get a mortgage. I heard they was dishing out council mortgages left right and centre up there. If you so much as parked on a yellow line they stuffed a mortgage application under your windscreen wipers. What did they say to me? Oh yes, you guessed it.

I'll follow the Sprightlys. Observe them. From a safe distance.

Comment

Sayers is a comically baleful disappointed copper. The ultimate Ogre-Cop: racist, sexist, fascist and reactionary. From his bowler to his riding-mac to his moustache to his highly-polished shoes he embodies spleen and dodginess. He speaks like a quietly sinister sergeant-major.

Sugar and Spice by Nigel Williams

Carol is one of a party of young punk girls. She and her friend Sharon have been pursued by some boys, who are taunting Carol to take her clothes off. Sharon tells Carol she is making a spectacle of herself – and Carol turns on her friend in the following speech.

CAROL   Ah, leave off me Sharon. I wanner be me if you wanner know an' woss so wrong wiv vat. An' if you mus' know I like wearin' nice clothes an' I like the way boys look at me when I go down the schtreet an' I like to look sexy an' I like lipstick an' showin' meself off an' all that I enjoy it. O.K.? Thass wot I call livin' if you mus' know. An' I dunno 'ow long I'll be livin' 'fore I'm sick like yore ol' lady 'angin' rahnd ver launjrette an' waitin' up fer ol' man an' 'avin' Gawd knows 'ow many kids 'angin' rahnd me an' 'Mummy this' and 'Mummy that' my Gawd if you mus' know Sharon all my life all I fuckin' wanner do is shine up there like a dancer or sunnink. Like sunnink reely glamorous that everyone wants an' I can't see woss so wrong wiv vat. 'Cos I ain't gonner get no kitchen wiv pitcher winders an' some geezer wiv a pipe like you was on abaht am I now? I be lucky I get any bloke fer more'n two monfs togevver like *my* ol' lady I suppose an' if I get a bloke 'e'll be aht a' work or 'e'll set me ter the bleed'n game like *'er* I wouldn't be surprised but if you reely want ter now jus' fer now for this minute I wanner enjoy it. I wanner go up in a pile a smoke an' flames an' eye shadder an' levver shoes an' dancin' an' all that I'll go like them girls in the magazines Sharon an' you ain't goin' ter stop me. O.K.?

                                                            Act 2

Comment

This speech in the cockney vernacular reads almost like a foreign language, but it has a well defined construction and rhythm. Notice how some of the words when repeated are better spoken than at other times, according to the level of passion in the delivery. The absence of punctuation is also a part of the style – but in spite of this you can sense the character struggling to articulate her thoughts clearly.

Educating Rita by Willy Russell

Rita is a young, married, working-class hairdresser, who rebels against her circumstances, and decides to acquire a higher education. She's talking to Frank, her university tutor.

RITA   What? Do you mean like that working-class culture thing? I don't see any, y'know, culture. I just see everyone pissed, or on the Valium, tryin' to get from one day to the next. Y' daren't say that round our way like, cos they're proud. They'll tell y' they've got culture as they sit there drinkin' keg beer out of plastic glasses. They're not content with it, cos there's no meaning. They tell y' stories about the past, y' know, the war, or when they were fightin' for food an' clothin' an houses. Their eyes light up as they tell y', because there was some meanin' to it. But the thing is that now, I mean now that most of them have got some sort of house, an' there's food an' money around, they know they're better off but, honest, they know they've got nothin' as well. There's like this sort of disease, but no one mentions it; everyone behaves as though it's normal, y' know inevitable that there's vandalism an' violence an' houses burnt out an' wrecked by the people they were built for. There's somethin' wrong. An' like the worst thing is that y' know the people who are like supposed to represent the people on our estate, y' know the Daily Mirror an' The Sun, an ITV an' the Unions, what are they tellin' people to do? They just tell them to go out an' get more money, don't they? But they don't want more money; it's like me, isn't it? Y' know, buyin' new dresses all the time, isn't it? The Unions tell them to go out an' get more money an' ITV an' the papers tell them what to spend it on so the disease is always covered up. I'm just tellin' y' about round our way. I wanna be on this course findin' out. You know what I learn from you, about art an' literature, it feeds me, inside. I can get through the rest of the week if I know I've got comin' here to look forward to.

Comment

Rita is a lively observer of her world, and describes it with vivid insight. She has seen who's pulling the strings. The speech is not a lamenting 'downer', it's full of irony, humour and compassion and honest indignation. She bursts with vitality and raw intelligence. Though she has had little education, her vocabulary is excellent: she fountains out ideas and observations at breathless speed. A smart, sexy, brave and warm young woman. The locale is described as a university in the north of England, it could be anywhere from Nottingham to Newcastle, but seems more likely to be Lancashire or Merseyside. The accent must be scrupulously well done: it's her truth, her vocal identity, her prison.

6   Training at drama school

All training for the theatre is aiming to produce a person with all-round performing skills, equipped and ready to work in the world of entertainment. It is easy to understand this, but it's not so easy to evaluate the different elements of theatre training, and see just how they contribute to the making of that elusive thing, 'a compleat actor'.

I have always considered drama training to be based on simple precepts, for acting is not a complicated art. It may be difficult, but it is not complicated, and if it gets complicated there is something quite wrong. Above all acting is not an intellectual occupation, though a good mind is needed to respond imaginatively and practically to the work of authors and directors. An actor can wear his cap as an academic in private conversation as well as the next person, but once on stage the actor responds to the requirements of a scene being played, and works through from moment to moment. And the fact that you already have a good instinct for acting will probably have been the main reason why you passed your entrance audition for drama school.

What you will eventually be working towards is a fusion of instinct and technique, and training is very largely to do with improving technical skills. At drama school, there is constant attention to a student's control of both voice and movement, and the different departments work at developing a student's overall acting technique. The emphasis will be on developing an actor's mental and physical concentration, and giving him/her sufficient craftsmanship to sustain a performance.

Classes

The first term is always an unsettling time, and it generally takes a few weeks before students become familiar with each other, and work together effectively. Classes are carefully time-tabled throughout the day, and occasionally stretch into the evenings.

It is usual for a class to consist of between 12 and 16 students divided approximately equally between male and female, and this size of class is likely to be maintained throughout the training course until the finals period in the last two terms. The two-year diploma course student will, of course, join the finals group earlier than the three-year course student. But in the first term all students start from the base line, and take many classes, individual tutorials and work on production projects.

The classes will generally be in voice, movement, improvisation, dancing, fencing, mask-work, make-up and acting exercises. There will probably also be some classes in radio, television and film techniques and perhaps singing too, but by far the largest proportion of time will be allotted to the production exercise which is part of every term's work. Most classes last for an hour or perhaps an hour and a half. In the first term, rehearsals for the production project will usually be around two hours in length, but progressively more time will be spent on this aspect of the course as the student advances.

Ideally the classes support the work done on the production project and it is particularly valuable if there is strong liaison between voice and movement tutors with the director of a project – not least in helping students see how the instructional classes connect with their own performances.

If drama schools do not incorporate a stage management course, basic lectures and some participation in production work may take place in the senior terms. It is always useful for a student of acting to have some practical knowledge of stage management, helping him/her to appreciate the need for efficient technical support for any production. And it can be particularly useful to have some background in this area, as a first job may often be that of an 'acting ASM' – particularly if you join a small touring group or a Theatre in Education company.

The voice and the body

It's not much use thinking of the voice without the body, even though each is the subject of a separate training class. The days when the voice was trained to be a beautiful sound in itself are no longer with us; instead, the emphasis is on a more natural approach, with each actor discovering the true quality of his/her own voice, and extending its range as much as possible. After all, the voice is an actor's number one asset, and it will be in use all the time.

Posture and physical balance have a great deal to contribute to vocalisation, a point which is stressed in Cicely Berry's standard book, *The Voice and the Actor*, which is used as a basic text in drama schools. The use of the voice in conjunction with the body is an important feature of training, too, for when acting you will need to be physically free enough to do several things at once. But besides this more obvious point, there are subtler connections between voice and body: Cicely Berry observes that 'an introverted and thoughtful person often finds more difficulty in speaking and does not carry the thought through into the physical process of making speech'. She says, too, 'you have to relate the mental intention to the physical action'.

Most drama training works on the assumption that there is something called 'standard English', which is generally considered to be the 'straight' delivery of words without affectation or regional variation. This means that actors are expected to be able to control any regional or foreign accent which is natural to them, and deliver a text in what may best be called 'the classical style'. It doesn't mean that your regional accent is going to be bullied out of you, so that you are unable to use it ever again – on the contrary, your accent may in all probablity be your most interesting and valuable possession. And good voice training will make your natural delivery sound ten times better than when you first started training.

A word here about singing – some schools have courses in choral singing, and may also run individual classes; not all students are singers, obviously, but it is always a useful addition to other vocal training. And a trained singing voice is undoubtedly a valued asset – there may well be some competition for a place on singing tutorials.

The first production

The text for the first term's production will usually be selected for the purpose of getting a new group to work together rather than trying to go for detailed individual performances. The range is obviously very wide, and you may find yourself in a Greek tragedy, or even a modern 'exercise' play such as *Games* by James Saunders, where the student may add to the text by research material which can be incorporated in the project. Either way, the main intention will be to establish a way of working, and to begin assessing students' voice and movement abilities. The language of a classical play is challenging but it does give the student chance to see how early voice training can be used with a very demanding text.

Most of these exercises are double cast so that there are good opportunities for several readings of the main characters.

Depending on the school, a full term's work of ten to twelve weeks may be spent on one production project during the first term, with either a workshop or text study area at the end of the period. Later on there will be a regular division of the term into two projects.

The new student does not perform to audiences immediately, and the first term's production project will probably only be attended by staff teaching voice, movement and acting to enable individual assessments to be made on training.

Improvisation

There have been many books written about improvisation and if I were asked to choose just one it would be Keith Johnston's *Impro* which is straightforward, understandable, and theatrically aware. Nowadays, nearly every young person has probably had some experience of basic improvisation at their school or through the extensive TIE (Theatre in Education) tours.

In drama schools, improvisation is about finding a way of expanding the imagination and liberating the senses, which can get too confined if students work entirely from a text all the time.

The use of impro in training has gone through many phases; it still conjures up the traditional, hackneyed image of a student being asked to be a tree or an icecream. But it's possible to go way beyond these limited, obvious exercises, and impro can be immensely exciting for young actors, allowing them to grasp situations and emotions imaginatively, perhaps for the first time.

Here is an example of an impro exercise for two actors: 'An actor is asked to assume the character of a close family friend who arrives at the house with the news of the death of the wife's husband in an accident. He has hurried to get there and tell the wife before the police arrive.' This may prove more effective if the girl playing the wife has no idea of what the scene is going to be about. What an impro of this kind does is confront the actors with a situation where they have to be emotionally truthful. Without a text to assist them they may prevaricate too long before facing the brutal truth.

Improvisation can mean having the guts to experience anything which is asked of you. Can you truthfully become a child again? Improvisation should not, in any way, be confused with the rather general idea of 'making things up as you go along', which has no real purpose beyond that of entertainment. Improvisation, if used properly, is intended to seek out something in you, and hopefully find an imaginative and emotional response.

Acting exercises

Acting 'exercises' differ from improvisation in that students work in a less open-ended way; the aim is to follow the intentions and actions of a character in a particular scene, often quite minutely. Of all the classes this is closest to what happens in an actual rehearsal, since it is much more concerned with the technical means of presenting a character. And class work in this area is usually referred to as 'technique' or simply 'acting'.

For example, one exercise which I have used in class is a play called *Justice* by John Galsworthy. Here a single actor plays an imprisoned man, and performs in silence, and the scene culminates in an emotional breakdown where the prisoner beats on the door of his cell. Galsworthy gives very precise details on the dimensions of the cell, the things that are in it and the character's sequence of actions. The piece tests the actor's awareness and imagination to the full, but nevertheless makes precise demands on him: he must follow exactly what the author says.

Throughout drama school there will be continuous work on acting solo pieces, and both singing and acting tutorials are usually conducted on a one to one basis (more on tutorials in chapter 7).

Of course the student also needs to learn how to co-ordinate dialogue with all of the necessary actions and movements which are part of the natural traffic of performance, and learn about prop handling. Classes help the actor to gain confidence in dealing with many things happening at the same time, and this is an important part of student work.

Radio, television and film classes

Most schools now offer classes on radio, television and film techniques. Radio acting makes specific technical demands on an actor, and classes are usually held by professional tutors who have a wide experience of radio drama and its production. Getting used to acting with the voice only and knowing how to use the microphone are basic features of good radio technique.

Students may compete for the BBC Carlton Hobbs award which is given annually to two students from any of the drama schools; the award offers a six month contract with BBC radio, as well as guaranteeing that vital entry into British Equity.

The facilities available for television training differs from school to school; filming and television work is expensive to organise, and really there is not so much opportunity as one would like to see for students to gain experience in these vital areas. However, where facilities are available for use over short periods of time, the rudiments of camera acting are taught in a structured way. (Some schools have been able to co-ordinate work with the National Film School, where a script has been written for the personalities in a group and then filmed on location, and this worked effectively.) But it's true to say that most actors feel their drama school training has left them inadequately prepared for working in television and film by the time they graduate.

Your drama school experience

The work of a drama school is necessarily highly disciplined – and indeed self discipline is an essential requirement in all acting. It is possible, though, that in the early stages of training you may feel that all your creative skill is being stripped from you, and that the whole system is ganging up on you. It's certainly true that the pressure on you builds up as the terms go on – but training is *not* designed to destroy you, but to challenge you. Remember this when the pace hots up!

Students usually find that the first term's work is relatively gentle. At nearly all schools no stage performances will be seen by an audience until at least the end of the second term. Sometimes students get anxious about this, and believe they are not making audience contact early enough; but if you think about it, the reasoning is clear. Most of your technical tutors will be seeing everything you do, and deriving what they need to know from it; they don't want to find you confused by criticism from senior students which might not be helpful to you at this point.

Ultimately, there are things in your training which you will accept – and those you may reject. And this is true of all training in the arts because nobody – no tutor, no establishment, however excellent, can finally lay down rules. They can only suggest concepts and invite you to use them.

The drama school training will only lay the foundations and prepare you for the profession you are joining. You will know about using the voice and body and know how not to exhaust yourself. Good training is there to support you and help you grow as an actor – and usually, it works. And at the end of the day I have always found that the training programme is open to genuine ideas – in all the classes the aim is to build and shape the existing talent so that the actor can work effectively and truthfully when faced with any situation.

Finally, here are some reminders – it may sound like a do's and don'ts column, but these are important things to remember. So I'll just list them:

1 Don't be late – anywhere or for anything. Punctuality is not just a drama school fetish, it's preparation for a profession where time really does cost money.
2 Learn lines accurately – and always carry a pencil with you.
3 If you have a question about acting, think about it before you ask it.
4 Read newspapers, and don't assume that the whole world is as interested in acting as you are.
5 Don't neglect your health. And don't imagine that you are too sick to attend classes that you don't like.
6 Think about your appearance, and how you present yourself as a person.
7 Watch how other people behave; remember everything is useful to the actor.
8 Go the theatre whenever you can.

7 *The final year*

The final terms at drama school are vital and exciting. This is the time you have worked towards, when you will be working on the 'showcase' productions which will provide opportunities for you to be seen publicly. The last three months particularly are charged with electricity – and you are suddenly involved both in the throes of final productions and the 'business' of acting; it all comes together in a thrilling rush, and the time goes quickly. There don't seem to be enough hours in the day to do all the things you have to do, quite apart from your laundry!

'Showcase' productions

Depending on the school's theatre resources, a full term of productions may mean that at least three or more plays will be staged, giving agents, directors and casting pundits a chance to evaluate your work. Students may find themselves performing in final productions over two full terms, which means they have the opportunity to play twice as many parts, but this depends on the school's policy and how they think you have progressed. At this stage, too, the allocation of parts and the standard of performance is becoming a lot more competitive – a foretaste of the profession itself.

In many cases students will also tour in productions mounted by the school, and this gives good audience experience away from the greenhouse of school performances, where the people who sit in the audience are usually either professionally interested, or are fellow students and friends.

Any programme of final drama school productions will present a variety of styles and the casting is aimed at giving students a chance to do well in suitable roles. Naturally, with a cast of actors who are all approximately the same age, the casting of heavy character parts has to be considered very carefully, and of course not all plays are teeming with characters of similar age.

Both classical and contemporary plays will be chosen, but problems are often encountered with the modern play which frequently has a short cast list. A finals company usually means there are some fourteen or sixteen students, or more, to be placed. It is possible for two productions to be mounted so that numbers are divided – possibly four productions may be put on, if that is thought worthwhile. Arguably the modern play with a limited cast is more effective in drawing in professional agents and casting directors since there are fewer 'bit' parts for students to get lost in. (On the other hand, plays like Tom Stoppard's *Jumpers* or Max Frisch's *Andorra* offer good opportunities for large numbers of students.) Quite clearly the most important thing about final presentations is that the play suits the talent available in the group. Yet every now and again a student emerges who shows exceptional talent and it is quite natural that a drama school will make sure that his/her ability is given a good stretch in public with a major role, perhaps playing *Hamlet* or *Hedda Gabler*. Some students, there is no denying, are more charismatic and powerful on stage than others – and it is always very difficult for the system to be absolutely fair.

However, one thing worth mentioning at this point is that the larger parts are not always a guarantee of an agent's interest – quite often big roles will attract attention, but a student who has been very well cast in a smaller role may hit the mark just as effectively.

Many drama schools regard musical productions as a main attraction, and shows such as *Cabaret*, *Guys and Dolls* and *Chicago* often get presented very well, with good choreography and musical direction which supports the cast very well. The ability to sing and dance has become increasingly important in the profession nowadays, and there are few actors who don't possess some musical and dance skills. Productions such as *Oh, What a Lovely War* offer many opportunities for voice and body training to be displayed effectively, particularly as the quick character sketches in this show mean that an actor may play several parts in one evening.

Press notices are, however, exceptionally rare these days. Once *The Stage* covered all finals productions from the drama schools, but now they may write up a play perhaps once a year. This is a pity, as it means that students find it harder to get their names known, and it means they lose out on a degree of publicity.

The private tutorial

In the last terms of the diploma course students often find tutorials, where they are given opportunity to talk about work in progress, enormously valuable. The tutorial is completely distinct from an 'audition' class; the object of the tutorial is to help a student concentrate on speeches and scenes which may extend aspects of characterisation or improve his/her vocal range, and also to increase confidence. They are personal work-out sessions. Altogether, tutorials take place over a period of about twenty-four weeks in the last year of a course, and usually by the last twelve tutorials a student has a much clearer idea of what he or she is about.

Where the tutorial focuses on current productions, I have found that students will work hard on their performances and be open about their work and any problems they may be having with the characters they are playing. A director may have made it plain that he has a definite intention for a character, but the student may not always see this straight away. Discussing a character and finding an outline of what is required in a half hour tutorial can save a lot of time on a tight rehearsal schedule.

But a tutorial need not be directly connected with a production in rehearsal. The student may want to find out more about the kind of parts he/she may play in the future, or indeed may have played during the time already spent at drama school. Perhaps certain parts played in the past have not succeeded, and it may be possible to investigate why. It is common for students to return to a part that has given them many ideas, and to rework a passage fruitfully. And in tutorials there is opportunity to take well judged risks – by which I mean being unafraid of going for the character and seeing where it leads – even with well known speeches. Some students will use the time to try out major speeches they have never attempted before, and find out where this may take them. So the tutorial is a place for ideas as well as practice, and if they are well used they can help an actor to be more objective about the craft.

Agents

Drama school productions are staged with an awareness of the kind of demands the profession will make, and students are naturally anxious to be seen in the final production by people who're likely to offer them work. Unfortunately, it is often difficult to get agents to attend these productions. Most drama schools final productions are staged over a similar sort of schedule, which means agents are asked to see students' work over a fairly compressed period.

Agents are notified of performances by the schools, and they also receive hundreds of letters from students inviting them to see particular performances. Remember, though, that badgering agents is quite useless; if they want to come they will come, but telephoning them and overselling yourself can be just as useless as not letting them know that you're alive and working. It will be the same story for many moons to come. Most of the drama schools now include a presentation of auditions for agents and managements at the end of the final term, in addition to the finals productions. This means that students then have the chance to present themselves as they would at a working audition, and this is often quite a good place to attract attention.

Although an agent may be very impressed by the talent he sees, there are practical difficulties which affect how much agents can do for young actors. The whole thorny question of Equity membership is linked with the step from drama school to agent's office – and indeed applies equally at the audition for the first job. But the positive interest of an agent is some quarantee that your work is not passing by unnoticed.

An agent looking at a student actor makes a reasonable commercial judgement; he considers whether a decision to take on an actor will be financially justified. Agents don't want deadwood and if they are interested in you it is because they feel they can sell you into the market, so that you can go on and make money both for yourself and them. They are not artistic philanthropists, but business people who are necessary to the profession. If that makes the agent sound unpleasant it is only because you are still seeing the profession through rose-coloured spectacles.

As a student in your last term you will begin to send out letters and photographs of yourself to all possible valuable contacts. Who are these? Well, the agents and the casting directors are one thing, then there's an amorphous list of anyone who seems to be connected with theatre, film and television. If any professional person has shown an interest in your work don't let it go, but try to cultivate their interest, however tenuous it may seem – you will soon know if it's going to be any use for the future.

In the first place you are your own agent. You are entering the market for the first time when you write a letter about yourself to either agent, casting director, producer or director. If an agent is interested in you he may well have useful comments on the photo you send of yourself, on your style and how you present yourself. Remember this will be a professional opinion from someone who is interested in the qualities you now have to offer, so bear such comment well in mind. The drama school will give you some advice on when and where to write to, and how you organise your letters, but outside advice is very important in helping you to see yourself in perspective.

Letters and the curriculum vitae

Writing letters about yourself is never easy – we tend either to say too much or too little. Nobody wants a florid letter from someone they have never seen before but as an actor your style and personality must come through sufficiently – a bare list of parts played won't convey much. Prepare details on a separate sheet of paper: your name, height, colouring, and the parts you have played in training. The accompanying letter needs to be personal and brief and should certainly not be sycophantic or name dropping. If you have particular skills like dancing, singing, fencing, acrobatics, or mime, be sure they are on this information sheet. I've even known fire eating, sword swallowing, skiing and judo to be useful, and they are certinly eye-catching – but be sure you really can do what you claim!

Photographs

Photographs are all-important. It's very difficult, though, to say what the right kind of photograph is, for obviously actors are very different, but remember that a good photograph is not necessarily an art photograph. The main thing is that it needs to look like you! Not everyone suits the same kind of photographic style, and it may take several tries before you find a picture that eventually gets you noticed. You will probably, therefore, end up with a selection of varying pictures which could well be useful. Getting a good set of prints is not cheap, although there are less expensive rates for students and most actors have a stock of postcard size prints that they can send off at the merest rumour of work. You will need to send a photograph to *Spotlight*, too. Quality in photographs costs money but it is an outlay that is never wasted for casting directors and producers do look at volumes of *Spotlight* repeatedly.

In recent years, photographs of newcomers to the profession have been put together in a volume expressly produced for that purpose, by *Spotlight*. The drama school will know about this, and make sure your picture is sent at the right time before you finish training.

Equity

We have already mentioned Equity, and for a number of reasons the entire question of how to enter the actors' union needs discussion at this point. Briefly, the organisation British Actors' Equity exists so that only bona fide members of the profession may apply for work: and those members must abide by the contractual rulings established by the Union in negotiation with managements in theatre, television and film. Equity is important in that it fights for improvements and fairness in pay and working conditions, and with over 44,000 members competing for probably some 5–7,000 jobs in any given working week, it tries to ensure that the work goes to professionally accredited people, those with training or suitable professional experience. Equity entry is of crucial concern to the large numbers of trained and talented drama school finalists seeking to enter the business every year. Membership of Equity, then, is no guarantee of employment – it simply gives the member a chance to be considered for the work that is available. No new actor should expect more. There are those who think that all drama students who graduate from drama school should be given an Equity card when they receive their diploma; to me, this is naive.

The present situation in 1990 is that would-be members can become provisional members by the following means; by being offered an engagement by any company or management which operates under the "Quota" system by agreement with Equity and the Theatre Managers' Association. That is, the employer will have places for a very small number of newcomers to the profession who are not yet union members. On taking up the job, the applicant will be granted provisional membership of Equity. The employers with a quota will mainly be Regional Repertories, children's theatres, touring companies, theatre-in-education, or young people's theatre companies, and strangely, the Royal Shakespeare Company at Stratford and Chichester Festival Theatre. There is no quota for the West-End Theatre, The National Theatre, television, commercials, films or radio. Those with training in other performance skills, variety, singers and dancers, should consult Equity about the means whereby they could qualify for membership. Summer seasons, pantomine and certain Fringe or small-scale companies also have a quota for performers and assistant stage managers and acting ASMs.

In addition to the quota system, Equity have compiled a "Graduate Register". The drama student, on successfully completing an acting or stage management training course at an NCDT accredited school registers with Equity, thereby becoming eligible for membership of the union if offered an engagement in any of the areas of work listed above.

It's tough to get into the union, and it's tough to earn a living in the profession. An Open Sesame to all comers would make it even tougher. The ball is not with the union or the performer but with those who fund the Arts. A determined, skilful young actor can get an Equity card and a first job. What comes after is the problem.

8　*The new actor*

Once you have left drama school your attention will be on the immediate problems of survival and making progress with your work. Most new actors have tremendous optimism, as indeed they must, for without belief in themselves training is just a huge waste of time.

Remember that drama school has only *prepared* you to work. Your diploma is a mark of that preparation – nothing more and nothing less. Clive Swift, in his admirable and essential book *The Job of Acting* says that when you were at drama school 'you were a big fish – now you're a tiddler'. But being in an overcrowded profession doesn't mean that you won't be considered. New faces are arriving all the time and in some cases actors make a quick start with a first job or they may have a relatively long wait before they get off the mark. This is true in more ways than simply obtaining an Equity card.

If you are fortunate enough to have secured an agent you will have someone with whom you can talk. Your agent will want you to be working, but they cannot perform miracles for you. It will be up to you to write constantly and make contacts everywhere and you will largely be responsible for yourself. You always have your agent to refer to should anyone make you an offer.

If you have had problems finding an agent, you might consider the possibility of applying to join a co-operative where actors work together and run their own agency. These can offer real support to new actors seeking their first taste of work and such co-ops do show enormous interest in the work of drama students in their last term. It's difficult to evaluate how successful such co-ops are but many do seem to gain work on a fairly reasonable basis for their members, and they are certainly worth considering.

Most students find that the first job does eventually come along, and even that elusive Equity card is attainable. Your first Equity card will be a provisional one; to become a full member you need to have worked for at least 30 weeks, not necessarily consecutively. Nevertheless, it's only realistic to assume that you may face longish periods of unemployment and to be prepared to deal with this constructively.

Isolation is one of the biggest problems for the unemployed actor, for acting is something which needs communication with others. The actor is dependent on the stimulus of other faces and voices. Quite a number of new actors form small fringe groups and work in plays on a profit sharing basis – and work opportunities may grow from such schemes. Small, little-known groups don't generally muster a large audience, of course, but they are often a good way of commanding interest from future employers. Certainly the new actor should never remain idle but create chances wherever possible. This may sound like cold comfort when you're desperately hoping for something to come along and get you going – but continuing your work and maintaining skills is vitally important. Above all you need new audience experience now you are out of drama school. And, although nobody wishes to be exploited with low wages and very difficult conditions, it is frankly better to find the ways and means of presenting yourself somehow, than not perform at all. The new actor is generally operating in top gear and if this momentum is stopped it can be very damaging to the morale and can result in an actor's technicals skills going rusty – something to be avoided at all costs.

To speak of further training programmes now may sound like a mere desperate remedy, but it doesn't mean anything as arduous or as expensive as the full training of your drama school. Actors who are serious about their work always look on the voice and movement class as an important part of their life. *It is*, and keeping yourself in trim is very important when you're not working. A ballet dancer who does not practise every day loses a lot of skill, as does a musician. The actor is no different, although for some reason it is often thought that you are somehow ready to act, magically, the moment you enter a stage door. Look after yourself, and particularly your voice and your memory, for without these you are dead meat.

So much of professional life is spent in the competitive atmosphere of interviews and auditions that a chance to work on themselves constructively and together is something actors relish. Since 1980 professional training courses have proliferated and many can be found in and around London. All of them take the working actors' problems into account and attempt to create classes which can make free hours both disciplined and profitable.

The Actors' Centre in Covent Garden has functioned since 1980, and offers a variety of professional classes in a relaxed atmosphere. It also caters for those who want more intensive sessions. For movement and dance, the Pineapple Studios in the same part of town seems to be one of the best there is, though it is not intended primarily for dancers and actors – people from all sorts of professions come along to keep fit. RADA holds regular annual classes for the professional during vacation periods; they offer refresher classes in both voice and movement which many actors find extremely valuable.

Everything in this chapter may seem terribly grey and pessimistic, but the truth is that acting is probably the most optimistic of all professions – it is the nature of actors to hope. However tough things seem, it's vital that you should keep your spirits up, and remember that acting *is* an art and a thrilling one – though sometimes when you are struggling with the frustrating process of building a career, this can all get a bit obscured.

Conversations

The following conversations with a handful of actors centred mainly on their attitudes to drama training, and their opinions about the audition system.

Different generations are well represented here, from the newest professional at the beginning of her career to two who have been in the business for the last forty years. Interestingly enough, having once entered the profession itself, age ceases to be a barrier, for actors of any age may easily teach each other something and share emotions honestly.

All the actors interviewed seemed to feel, and state quite naturally and simply that there was really nothing else for them to do but act. None of them were particularly concerned with 'glamour'. What does stand out is that everyone believes that the profession, its standards and its aims, *matter*, and they all feel an excitement about the job of acting. All are concerned with practical issues such as the accessibility of the union to those who are coming into the profession and the need to find sensible ways of selecting actors for parts. They voice real criticism of the way things are managed both artistically and in terms of employment.

I wish to express my sincerest thanks to 'all those taking part', and for giving me their time. For fairly obvious reasons the conversations begin with one of the most recent entrants to the profession, and ends with the two most senior actors.

Jenny Funnell

Trained at Webber Douglas Academy. She won the 1984 Carlton Hobb's Radio Award at the BBC and completed a contract with the Repertory Company in July 1985. Prior to this she played Ophelia in both *Hamlet* and *Rosencrantz and Guildenstern are Dead* for Theatr Clwyd and on tour. Also played Anna in *Self-inflicted Wounds* by Tom Kempinski.

A.R.   Although you won the BBC radio competition for a place in the BBC Repertory company straight from drama school, you decided to start your career by playing Ophelia in Hamlet at Theatr Clwyd. Do you feel that was the right way round for you?

J.F.   Yes, I do. I was terribly excited of course, to win the BBC competition but I do feel that going into the threatre first was a great help. Doing Ophelia on stage before taking up the BBC contract meant that I went there with a little track record – I'd been blooded, if you like, and it made the whole thing a lot better.

A.R.   Tell me about your audition to get Ophelia.

J.F.   Well, I'd thought a lot about the part. I knew I wouldn't play her as a wimp and the whole audition was based on the speech where she goes mad – the flowers, rosemary for remembrance and the whole bit. George Roman read me and after I'd done the first reading he asked me about my own attitudes to the part and then told me his as a director, which were completely different. So I asked if I might go through it again and try some of the ideas he talked about.

A.R.   Did you find it easy to take direction from someone whom you didn't know?

J.F.   Yes. Because that's where I realised that the drama school training helped a lot. When you're training you have ideas shoved at you continually and are expected to change quickly – which is a very good thing.

A.R.   Did your experience at drama school come as a great surprise to you?

J.F.   Well, it did really. I hadn't a clue what was expected. I hadn't done 'drama' at school, thank God, so I was completely open coming straight from school. There were a lot of people older than me with more experience of life.

A.R.   Do you think it a good idea coming into drama training direct from school?

J.F.   It was for me. I'd been trying to get into training since I was fourteen.

A.R.   That's a bit early.

J.F.   I realise that now. But it's all I ever wanted to do. Most of my family is in the medical profession and doctors always seem to be full of drama. My twin sister is a nurse and I suppose all the blood and thunder of things took me a different way. It was three years later that I did finally audition, at seventeen. I did the well trodden path, with Phoebe in *As You Like It*.

A.R.   Did you ever play that part?

J.F.   No. When the school did do a production I played Celia.

A.R.   So you played quite a bit in the classics during training.

J.F.   I finished by playing Isabella in a production of *Women Beware Women* in a 1950's style which may have helped when I came to my Ophelia, which was loosely based on a Princess Di concept. But I think my most rewarding part at drama school was Carol in David Storey's play *Sisters*.

A.R.   Do you have a preference for classical acting or the modern theatre at the moment?

J.F.   I always wanted to do the heavy parts. But I love playing comedy and then I'm not very tall. Perhaps radio will allow me to play all the unsuitable roles that I can't do visually in the theatre, where it's just the voice and the character.

A.R.   What did you do for the BBC competition?

J.F.   We had to do four pieces with different accents and a piece of real sight reading of poetry without any time to look at it. And then six of us did an extract from *Great Expectations*.

A.R.   What about television training? Did the drama school include any of that?

J.F.   Oh, yes. We did a fortnight's production which I enjoyed immensely. I hated seeing myself at first – we all did. But it wasn't as bad as I thought it might be.

A.R.   Do you think drama school should include more training for television and film?

J.F.   Definitely more for television. But I prefer the stage really. I like the feeling of doing it 'now' rather than it being a recording.

A.R.   Can you say what the best things are from your drama school experience and what has been of most value to you during your first year in the profession?

J.F.   The voice teaching and knowing how to keep yourself ready vocally; that really is the most important thing, which you don't realise when you start out. And singing is part of that too – I didn't sing before I went into training even though I am musical and play both the piano and the flute. But being trained to use your singing voice is really good. Perhaps some of the voice teaching was repetitive in the second term, but when there was a change in voice tutor who developed pieces of your own choice rather than just vocal exercises the whole thing came alive and interesting. I think that drama school stops you playing safe too early on in life and encourages you to take risks. I think if you don't go to train and still find your way into the profession some of the essential things you need to know about and be able to do will take that much longer to achieve.

Amanda Root

Trained at Webber Douglas Academy. Her first job was in 1983 with the Leeds Playhouse Company, playing Essie in *The Devil's Disciple* by Bernard Shaw. She followed this by joining the Royal Shakespeare Company on tour playing Juliet and later repeating this performance in the Other Place at Stratford upon Avon. While in Stratford she also played Jessica in *The Merchant of Venice* and Moth in *Love's Labours Lost*. Recent work includes a television play *This Lightning Always Strikes Twice* and the play *Dragons*.

A.R.   Were you surprised how soon you got into the RSC – and that you have now ended up after only just over a year and a half in the profession playing Juliet and Hermia?

AMANDA   I was amazed! It all happened so quickly – sometimes I think it may have been too quickly. The only other experience I had was playing Essie in Shaw's play *The Devil's Disciple* at Leeds . . .

A.R.   For which you auditioned with your drama school prepared pieces or by reading for the part?

AMANDA   No. By reading for the part and an interview. My first audition, as such, was actually for John Caird who wanted me to do a piece of Juliet. I only had twenty four hours' notice and then I sat up all night learning a speech and then dried flat at the audition. So they asked me to go away and come back again in a week which gave me breathing space and time at least to learn it properly.

A.R.   What speeches did you choose to do?

AMANDA   For Juliet I did 'Thou knowest the mask of night is on my face' and for Hermia I did the 'puppet' speech. You know, all aggro and spirit. And that got me into the last three so I had to do it all again at the Barbican which I think was to see if I could fill that theatre with enough presence and vocal range. It was all terrifically exciting and when I got the parts I could hardly believe it.

A.R.   On reflection, do you think the audition process is a good one?

AMANDA   Well, I haven't had enough experience of it yet. Having been lucky with the only real audition I did which was for the RSC, I can't really complain about it. But I think it's probably different for different people. I mean, sight reading is another thing and not everyone is good at that, but it helps if you are. My audition for Leeds was a sight reading job and it's something that you get from drama training – work that helps you cope with the sight reading at an audition – yes. I mean, radio work classes helped a lot in that respect.

A.R.   Did you have any experience of a kind that helped you before you came to drama school?

AMANDA   It's very daunting to have to go to an audition for the first time in your life. And you're not sure what is expected. I mean I had no idea that by doing 'I left no ring with her' by Viola I was doing something that must have been heard a hundred times that day – I had no idea.

A.R.   Had you always wanted to be an actor?

AMANDA   Well, yes, I think I must have done. I used to watch television and think 'I want to do that'. All very clichéd but true. At school I did English and Art, and looked at theatre design in art – it was all pointing the same way, really. Of course at school they always tell you that you should do a secretarial course, which was absolutely dreadful, and they put you off the idea of a career in the theatre just as much as they can.

A.R.   Is classical training the most important ingredient for today's student? You have come into a classical company which makes sense of that training but what other ingredients do you think vital?

AMANDA   I think in a company like the RSC you are privileged and you go on learning all the time. It's like an extension of your training, with bigger resources and bigger audiences with which to practise and share the way you work. That's what's so marvellous. Particularly in doing a great part like Juliet which we toured in all kinds of places before coming here to the Other Place venue.

A.R.   As a new young actor do you find that at Stratford you become part of a house style?

AMANDA   I don't think there's a style of voice, thank goodness. But there is the chance of working with Cicely Berry, who is so wonderful at adding in a positive, performance orientated way to all the things you have learnt about voice. And of course holding together a part like Juliet with long gaps between the performance nights and no real rehearsal in between is difficult to do – that can be rather hairy. Sometimes you're a week away from the last performance you gave and then find yourself out there – so that the voice and understanding of the part does need constant refreshing. That's the big lesson. One is always in a state of learning – if you stop learning it's hopeless, I feel.

A.R.   What do you feel about working in the more modern style of play after your classical work with Stratford?

AMANDA   Yes. There's lots of new plays being written that I look at and say 'Oh yes – there's lots of opportunities there'. I mean, *Sugar and Spice* for example by Nigel Williams; I'd love to have a go at doing the part of Sharon sometime. I think anything that is well written – that's important.

A.R.   Being well written?

AMANDA   Yes. Perhaps doing Shakespeare spoils you for that, but I think having a text that is good is important. We ought to do more modern work at drama school, as well as the classics. I remember doing the Stoppard play *Undiscovered Country* which was a great help and drama school needs to do more of that sort of thing. We need to be of 'now' and maybe that's a better way of playing 'then'.

A.R.   The past is often reflected by something called documentary drama, which uses improvisation before arriving at a script in its final state. What do you feel about that?

AMANDA   Yes. I loved all that. But improvising round a text and its written characters, finding out about their intentions is very exciting too. When I went to drama school it was all very new to me so I didn't have any real comparisons to make – which is a good thing. I think you have to see what the system is and then see how you get it to work for yourself.

A.R.   Are there aspects of training that you find to have been missing or superficial now that you have had the chance of putting your technical skill to the test?

AMANDA   I think the training has been basically good. I do think there's a greater need for other aspects to be included – like the Alexander technique, which helps with your body control. For example, I had no idea about playing scenes on a raked stage, which can throw your weight out in placement very considerably. Being technically aware of your body is very important and the more drama school does about that the better.

Kenneth Branagh

Trained at RADA. Played Judd in *Another Country* as almost his first job, following this with *Francis*, the title role in a new play at Greenwich Theatre. Joined the Royal Shakespeare Company playing Henry V, Laertes and King of Navarre in *Love's Labours Lost* at Stratford upon Avon and in the Barbican Theatre, London. Television includes *Too Late to Talk to Billy*, *To the Lighthouse* and *The Boy in the Bush*.

A.R.   Did you go straight from school into actor training?

K.B.   Yes. I thought it was better going to drama school direct rather than via a university and if you're going to act I think that's the way. Before going to RADA I had been encouraged at my school in school plays, which included *Oh, What a Lovely War*. I also did a great deal of amateur acting with the Progress Theatre in Reading.

A.R.   Was getting into RADA an audition process that you enjoyed, coming as you did straight from school.

K.B.   Well, I must admit there's a bit of me that thrives slightly on the exam syndrome – something that gets the adrenalin flowing rather like 'first nights'. A bit gladiatorial, I suppose one might say – a sort of us and them feeling. But getting into RADA was quite a searching process and I remember doing four one-hour work sessions with some of the tutors there, including the Principal, before finally being accepted for the three-year course there. Now I think that's the right way to get to know the kind of talent there is, rather than a straight knock-down audition. It was more humane.

A.R.   Once you had been through the three years what did you find had developed most for you as an actor?

K.B.   Leaving drama school you do feel as though you are really in control of your destiny. You can at least organise your life around your aims and ambitions. I must have prepared some twelve pieces for possible auditions.

A.R.   That's quite a lot – quite a programme of work. As a young actor you obviously went for a great deal of variety in characters and accents.

K.B.   Oh, yes . . . my American piece, my Irish and the modern funny and modern serious – the same with the classics. Always varied. As an auditionee I knew I worked best if I attempted something outrageous so I prepared Lord Foppington from *The Relapse* and you just have to let go with his Lordship otherwise there's no point to it. I also put together an adaptation of my own from *The Pickwick Papers* in which I took on four characters all travelling in a coach together, then mixed it with the narration, rather as they did with the production of *Nicholas Nickleby*. I enjoyed doing this because it took people by surprise.

A.R.   Did you get your first job from an audition?

K.B.   Well, my first job came during four weeks of my last term at RADA when I had applied and been chosen for a television play called *It's Too Late to Talk to Billy* which was set in Belfast – which is where I came from originally. So the accent was no problem and I was the right age. It gave me a temporary Equity card – mind you they took it away again as soon as I had done the four weeks work.

A.R.   And when you went back to RADA you finished your final term with what?

K.B.   I played Hamlet, which was a wonderful chance. It got me noticed here although I think the one-man show I did outside on my own was the real deciding factor with the RSC.

A.R.   What was the one-man show about?

K.B.   I took the dramatic poem 'Maud' by Tennyson – all fourteen hundred lines – and learnt them and presented them working with two friends, a designer and a lighting man. It was a great experience.

A.R.   Your first stage part was in something quite different from the classical roles, wasn't it?

K.B. Yes. I had the chance to audition for the transfer to London cast of *Another Country* which requires young actors to play seventeen-year-olds. Again, there were difficulties with Equity when I was selected and the whole thing had to go to arbitration because the company stood out for the casting it wanted.

A.R. Equity seems to have been prominent in your career very early on. Do you think the entry into Equity for drama students is unfairly organised?

K.B. I do think there should be better arrangements for students leaving to audition and get provisional cards and not always be intimidated by the 'Equity only' requirement at auditions. If not a provisional card another way of permission to be seen properly at meaningful auditions. After all, having a card isn't having work – you still have to get that on your own.

Pamela Salem

Trained at the Central School of Speech and Drama in London, which was followed by repertory theatre in various parts of the country, national tours, and theatre abroad, Vienna, Stockholm, the Caribbean, and a Britsh Council tour of *Betrayal* in Switzerland and Portugal.

Her recent television credits include leads in the series *Buccaneer*, *The Professionals*, *The Consultant*, *Into the Labyrinth*, *Lytton's Diary*, *Magnum*, *Seagull Island*, and her film credits include *The First Great Train Robbery*, *The Bitch*, Morecambe and Wise's *Night Train to Murder*, Miss Moneypenny in *Never Say Never Again*, *Universal City*, *After Darkness*, and she has just completed *Salome*, playing Herodias.

A.R. Would you say that things have changed a great deal from the days when you finished your drama school training at Central in 1966?

P.S. I think the profession has changed because the opportunities are different. First of all I'm absolutely against having the controlled entry into Equity. It is much worse these days than it was in 1966. Things should be made easier; after all actors come from all walks of life and we shouldn't keep them out. They should have a provisional card for Equity at the beginning of their career.

A.R.   You mean that drama students who are graduating from training should have the chance to join Equity?

P.S.   Certainly they should. Actors who train and go to drama school are usually on grants from local education authorities and to deny them the chance to join the profession – or at least compete properly – is ridiculous. After all, becoming a provisional member of Equity doesn't give them work, it merely gives them the opportunity to work in the career for which they have trained.

A.R.   We've plunged in with the practical details rather than training itself. Do you think that training is essential?

P.S.   Some kind of training is vital. I'm not so sure about drama schools, sometimes. The voice and movement work is very important but the professional requirements have changed, particularly in respect of film and television and there should be more training in this area. We had next to none when I was at drama school and young actors need to know more about what will be expected of them on film sets and television studios. And young actors have a greater instinct these days for film than they do for the stage, though this is not to say that stage training is not equally important; nevertheless as working actors we are getting more and more camera conscious in our acting and will continue to do so.

A.R.   Would you say that with so much emphasis on film and the camera, theatre training is becoming less important?

P.S.   No. We have to remember that many of the new actors will find their first work in the theatre. I think there are questions of style and dimension which come down to what type of theatre you are talking about. Many actors start in the fringe productions – in small theatres almost as intimate as television, material concentrating on highly detailed reality. Personally I'm not sure that highly detailed reality is what the theatre is truly about. The film does that so much better.

A.R.   The theatre is always larger than life, isn't it?

P.S.   Much. Which is why I think naturalistic plays with domestic situations need very careful handling. They are so like the television it's sometimes hard to see why they are being done on a stage. Yes, the stage is larger than life and it is about emotions that are big enough to wrap round you. The theatre is at it's best being spectacular and for experimental new plays – I certainly don't think the theatre should be like television.

We have problems on British television because our theatrical tradition gets in the way, so that characters talk too much, as though the medium is only half way from the stage. Quite often the stage element in TV plays sounds phoney. And all of this is a problem facing the new actor coming out of training.

A.R.   What do you think existing kinds of drama training do for the new actor?

P.S.   It centres the classical traditions in a way that no other kind of training can do. Drama school isn't going to teach anybody to act but it does give the vital techniques with which to act and gives you a chance to make mistakes, experiment and find out about yourself. But it should do more these days about practical matters – like the tax system and keeping yourself together while you're out of work and waiting for the next job, for that is fifty percent of what you'll be doing. And, of course, working with professional directors who won't say things like 'Your uvula isn't relaxed enough', but simply 'I can't hear you'.

A.R.   Getting into drama school is highly competitive and requires an audition and interview. Later on in the profession itself the process goes on at a different level. What do you think of the audition system generally?

P.S.   Awful – but what else can one do? For drama school it is the first taste of things to come and on the whole a good thing. Later in the profession it can vary a great deal. If you feel you have done well at an interview and everyone seems to like you it is quite likely to find that you haven't got the part. A cold and depressing interview can mean the reverse.

A.R.   Have you had that experience recently?

P.S.   I had an alarming reading for an Agatha Christie film where I was given several sheets of script to sight read without any logical link up in the scenes being read and no-one to read with, except an office assistant who couldn't read dialogue. What was interesting was the director who said to everyone auditioning – 'Look I know you are all good actresses. I just want to get the looks right'. The audition was simply acting by numbers.

A.R.   And you got the part?

P.S.   I got the part.

A.R.   What would you say is the toughest time after finishing drama school?

P.S.   The second year. The first year you're running on adrenalin and you're going to take on the world. The second year you realise that it's terribly, terribly hard. I remember when I left Central School in 1966 they said the average life for a woman in the theatre was three years and seven for a man before giving it up. So after four years I thought I'd survived.

A.R.   What do you feel about actors keeping themselves in step with training once they are in the profession?

P.S.   I think it's very important but I think a lot of us are very lazy. But you do need to do good voice and movement workouts – it's like going back to the keyboard for a musician. Americans are much better at this than we are. They enquire more. They are not content to just rest on their laurels. On the whole we are, until suddenly panic reigns and we must rush to a class again and limber up.

A.R.   So in a way we never stop training.

P.S.   And that means in a way one never stops working.

Patrick Ryecart

Trained at Webber Douglas Academy. First major West End role was playing Marchbanks to Deborah Kerr's Candida in 1977. Co-presented the play *The Beastley Beatitudes of Balthazar B* as well as starring in it. He followed this with Jack Absolute in *The Rivals* at the National Theatre and David Mamet's *A Life in the Theatre* with Freddie Jones at the Open Space. His television includes Romeo in the BBC Shakespeare series and most recently *Silas Marner*. His latest theatre has included Oberon/Theseus in *A Midsummer Nights Dream* and the fascinating double Hugo/-Frederick in Anouilh's *Ring Round the Moon* at the open air theatre in Regent's Park, London.

A.R.   What do you recall that's most important from your days as a drama student – which are about ten years ago?

P.R.   I can remember everything. And I've rejected nothing, but the things that happen when working expand the horizons and the understanding. The absolute discipline of drama training is one of the major things that helps you all the time. I had already been part of the theatre working as an ASM at the Cambridge Arts Theatre, not with the University but with the

Prospect Theatre Company at a very exciting time. When I came to train properly I was already aware of the professional background.

A.R. Did you go into drama training straight from school?

P.R. Well, no. I tried an abortive term at Durham University Drama Department and that made me realise even more that I wanted the real thing; by then I had, in any case, worked the ASM stint and I didn't need theory; I wanted practice.

A.R. Would you say that drama school is necessary if you have already made some professional contact?

P.R. I think the whole thing of being a student over three years – the camaraderie if you like, is vital. The sharing and growing up without much money and finding a belief in yourself and the work. The student life is very important – in perspective.

A.R. You went to Hornchurch Rep for your first job?

P.R. That's right. It was the part of Sabbo in *Rope*; mind you, I had been offered two leading roles at other reps that couldn't give me the vital Equity card – so Sabbo it was.

A.R. So you would say the audition work proved successful?

P.R. Not auditions as such. People had seen me in my drama school finals. No. I'm quite hopeless at the set auditions, I think. I know it's silly but I find it hard to take them seriously and really concentrate and not be distracted by the local cat cleaning himself on a window ledge or some such thing. I nearly always dry. Or did.

A.R. Your first big stroke of fortune was playing Eugene Marchbanks in Shaw's *Candida* with Deborah Kerr in the West End.

P.R. And that was a tense business. It took several months for that to come home and safe. It was then that I became fully aware of how your personality is really at stake. That the audition process was one that examined you totally – your private behaviour as well as your theatrical ability, the two feeding into each other to find a way to suit the requirements of the part and the particular aspects that were being looked at by the director, Michael Blakemore. So achieving Marchbanks was a gradual and thoughtul affair – I remember being taken aside by the director and given a whole day after we had been rehearsing for two weeks and simply talking together about the play and about ourselves which was the real making of the part over the next weeks of final rehearsal. The audition had been one thing, the working through the part another – which is something it seems very hard for the audition process to make proper allowance for.

A.R.   Would you say that this way of casting and rehearsal is a luxury almost exclusive to the major nationally subsidised companies like the National Theatre or the RSC?

P.R.   Usually, I suppose, but *Candida* and Marchbanks belonged to the commercial theatre – a straight West End run.

A.R.   Did that part lead to the next in any way?

P.R.   Yes, it did. Although the story of my doing *Balthazar B and the Beastly Beatitudes* is a bit strange inasmuch as I ended up playing the part that was completely opposite from the one I was originally intended to do. That had more to do with management and the presentation of the play to those who were backing it – so instead of playing Beefy, who is described as 'the world's most beatific observer' I played the opposite number who was 'the world's las shy elegant young man'. Which was right be had no resemblance to what is commercially thought of a typecasting in any way – it's just that the mixture was right with Simon Callow.

A.R.   And later – much later at the National Theatre playing the young Captain Absolute – did that grow out of being seen in these performances?

P.R.   I'm sure it did. The NT is obviously interested in new talent but also in staying power – track record in sustainment, as indeed they should. Playing a big classic like *The Rivals* is enormously demanding.

A.R.   Do you think typecasting is inevitable in one's early days as an actor?

P.R.   I think there is always an element of typecasting that is sensible, I mean it doesn't have to be restrictive. In any case one person's typecasting isn't always another's. But, yes – I read plays and I can see actors in the parts – I hope I can see what is suitable to their personalities. Perhaps that is why I'm not all that much attached to being part of a permanent company for too long – I get bored by being around in one place for too long. I think you need a great variety of experience to build your work and need to fail as well as succeed sometimes. New actors need to try and widen their range all the time and in the same breath find a way of being commercially as well as artistically viable. I have been very lucky; the right opportunities have come along and yet every time you take them you are looking forward immediately to the next challenge. I mean the most exciting moment of all is when you are actually chosen for a part – after that initial excitement it's a bit downhill – not because the work isn't marvellous but because the first challenge is the peak. I think everyone needs the director to be vitally interested in the work well beyond the first week of actual performance. In the West End there seems at the moment a tendency to rely too much on the goodwill of actors which is often accompanied by a failure to maintain a true interest in what is going on for the actor. Perhaps directors in particular need to realise how much their vitality means to the continuing performance – that it isn't enough to be left up on a stage merely doing it night after night.

A.R.   Is that something that you feel may come from the 'hothouse' atmosphere of drama school in the first place?

P.R.   Maybe it does. But it's no bad thing – we should take the two way traffic of actors and directors more seriously than we do. And a production should not just be a matter of getting a good notice and leaving it to go to seed slowly.

David Suchet

Trained at LAMDA. Has worked a great deal with the Royal Shakespeare Company playing the leading roles of Shylock in *The Merchant of Venice*, Achilles in *Troilus and Cressida*, Bolingbroke in *Richard II* and Iago in *Othello*. His performances on television have been as varied as Freud, and as Blott in Tom Sharpe's *Blott on the Landscape*. He won the BBC best radio actor award in 1979 for *The Kreutzer Sonata*. His films include *Song for Europe*, *Greystoke* and *The Little Drummer Girl*.

A.R.   Did you always want to be an actor?

D.S.   No. Originally I wanted to be a doctor like my father, but it was soon clear I didn't have the intelligence for that – that's to say I wasn't any good at mathematics and physics and that sort of thing.

A.R.   No actor seems to be. I wonder why?

D.S.   Stanislavsky says it's the multiplication table syndrome. He gives an example about lifting a heavy weight and doing a multiplication sum at the same time and says you can't do it. Well, I was one of the people who couldn't do it even if I wasn't lifting a heavy weight.

A.R.   You didn't do that exercise in drama school?

D.S.   Not that I can remember. I went to drama school having done all the correct things that drama students are supposed to ignore – like going to public school (Wellington) and dressing in conventional clothes. The teachers gave me a rough time for a couple of years because my student and acting image didn't fit. I still don't feel it's necessary to wear scruffy clothes to be an actor.

A.R.   Had any of these attitudes been generated by your first experience with the National Youth Theatre under Michael Croft?

D.S.   Not at all. I can remember doing *Bartholomew Fair* at the Royal Court Theatre with the NYT and seeing all the scenery and lighting down on the stage at the end of the last performance and thinking how exciting it was to belong to the world of make-believe.

A.R.   And was that your reason for becoming an actor?

D.S.   It was then. After that came my training at LAMDA and the realisation that make-believe or not, acting was hard work. And because, as I say, of my conventional background there seemed at the time a tendency to think of me as a reactionary young man.

A.R.   Did you think of yourself as a classical actor in those days?

D.S.   Certainly not. In fact I found Shakespeare very difficult to get on with and wasn't at all sure that I wanted to. So the first thing I did was to spend ten years with the Royal Shakespeare Company!

A.R.   In which you played a lot of leading parts, as the days went by.

D.S.   That's right. And I discovered the language and size of the plays in which I was working with all their complexities. You can't possibly hope to get that in your early days as a student. The real work of acting takes on a different dimension. It's not a matter of theorising – hard work never is. Acting can be both pleasure and torture – but it is not fun and people are sometimes more concerned with the image of being an actor 'at work' rather than just working.

A.R.   Can you say that your drama training has served you well?

D.S.   One of the great things about drama school is what you learn to reject as much as what you actually learn. When I visit drama schools now – and I firmly believe the professional actor is someone who should remain in touch with students – it's a matter of trying to help future actors to gain a clearer focus on the profession they are joining. There are so many things that matter. Health and stamina, plus a constant awareness of building the voice. Training is about trying to put the component parts together – the physical and the mental, working towards an agility in both.

A.R.   What would you advise the new actor or the student to concentrate on in terms of auditioning?

D.S.   My word of advice is this. Don't worry about going out there to give the greatest performance of any particular speech and then come away depressed because you know you've done it badly. I would say always remember that what is on show is oneself, not necessarily the ability to perform brilliant characterisations. The things to remember are the practical ones about yourself. 'Next please. Mr Suchet!' You go out there with trembling knees, and they are already noticing those trembling knees. The greatest acting role in an audition is to appear just to be yourself.

A.R.   Oscar Wilde said the most difficult pose was the natural one.

D.S.   Absolutely. And even more difficult in an audition situation where they are looking at your height, weight and how much stage you can fill by your very presence. Does he engage me? That is probably the most important question the panel are asking themselves. And the next thing will be 'what is his attitude to this audition – is it positive?' Always remember that they have asked to see you and that is what they want to do. So dress the part. Don't go along in a dirty T shirt and floppy gym shoes or try to over-impress or be antagonistic. But just remember that you are being judged even before you speak a word. This is the first big lesson to learn. The next important lesson is to never apologise for being there. The number of auditions I have taken and started with the familiar question 'what would you like to do?' And the reaction has been one of slight stuttering, saying 'Er, erm, . . . well . . . I'm sorry but er . . . well I've got two pieces that er won't take long. The first speech is from Shakespeare and it's taken from the Chorus in Henry . . . Henry V and the second piece I'd like to do is a contract if . . . if, that is, we have time.'

OK, by now you've lost valuable time and probably irritated the entire panel by dithering instead of being sure of what you're going to say, quite apart from getting on with the actual pieces you have learned.

A.R.   Of course you cannot teach confidence but you can teach a way of acquiring it. We always want to see and hear confident actors.

D.S.   Exactly that, although God knows confidence is difficult enough to hold on to. But you *do* have a right to be there and to be heard. Announce yourself clearly and think of what you intend to do. Take your time – and do it.

Linda Marlow

Trained at Central School of Speech and Drama. On leaving she joined the Repertory Company at Worthing and played a great deal on the repertory circuit. Since those days she has done a great deal of work with Steven Berkoff – particularly in his play for two people, *Decadence* which she has played in London, Los Angeles and Dublin. She co-founded, wrote and performed with a rock group in the early 70's called 'The Sadista Sisters'. In films she has recently completed a feature role in *Mr Love* for David Puttnam.

A.R.   What do think is the most important thing for an actor to keep uppermost in mind when working in the profession?

L.M   Gauging the kind of people you are going to meet in the way of giving you work. It is your personality and your personal care that is going to be noticed all the time. If you're up for a 'tart' part you must be prepared to present a flavour of the role as you see it. If it's a general audition, be prepared for anything; look good and concentrate like mad on your work – always do that anyway.

A.R.   Do you think actors need to keep in training once they have graduated from drama school?

L.M.   I think most actors are conscious of the need to keep in training. It's a very physically demanding business; dancing is a wonderful way of keeping in training and also gives you a bigger scope in theatre these days. I think dancers can teach actors a lot and vice versa.

A.R.   Have you done any drama teaching yourself?

L.M.   Yes. At the East 15 Drama School I have taken audition technique sessions, which was all fine and large but I encouraged them to write their own material as well as having stock pieces to do. Writing your own pieces can be very exciting – if you have a talent for writing – and can be more suitable to show off your personal talents. That and sight reading which is probably the most important thing of all. Auditioning makes me very nervous but sight reading – maybe because I'm better at it – inspires me with more confidence. In filming you have a lot of this to do where you read a script through once and then have go.

A.R.   In the theatre you've worked a lot with Steven Berkoff and his own plays. Has this been something special in acting for you?

L.M.   Yes. Very special. I know Steven's method of working very well now. We did *Decadence* in London and America together – and we've made a film for Channel 4 television. There is something very physical as well as verbally strong about Steven's plays. But I think it's always a case of what you bring to acting – bring to the parts that are being offered to you. When I did Nurse Ratchett in *One Flew Over The Cuckoo's Nest* up in Manchester I read the novel and found a speech in the book that was really wonderful on the character and I asked the director if I could read it for him. I got the job and the speech became included in the play itself. I think you do have to do your homework as an actor.

A.R.   There are not the chances around these days as there were some years ago. Do you think actors now leaving training face greater difficulties?

L.M.   Without doubt they do. When I got my first job out of training it was at Worthing in a juvenile leading role and I got my Equity card because I had been chosen. That doesn't happen any more with young actors coming out of drama school. Twenty years ago it was expected that if you trained you would surely be accepted into the membership of your trade union and be given the chance to compete for the roles that were suitable. It was the last days of the old tradition, I suppose and I'm glad I was lucky enough to be part of them. Now there is no guarantee that a career actually exists and Equity are not making it all any easier for the new young actors to establish themselves. And with the theatre running into difficulties about subsidy it's not getting any more hopeful.

A.R.   In fact the dream that we all had about Great Britain acknowledging it's theatre and funding it properly has suffered a lot of setbacks since the 'sixties'.

L.M.   Yes. I think the present Government has a lot to answer for. After all we knew that subsidy didn't exist to subsidise empty seats but rather the necessary and new ideas that were wanted at the time. That is what subsidy is really all about.

A.R.   So for new actors coming into the business of acting what do you advise as the best possible course of action?

L.M.   To be ready to work at all times. Auditions are a painful necessity of life and not a fair judgement on your career but you have to go through them. It's all experience and that's what you have to have a lot of before getting your own way about anything.

A.R.   Or 'you don't go through an experience; an experience goes through you'?

L.M.   True – like a dose of salts! But as to advice – well, don't just sit around waiting for the telephone to ring. Actors must be prepared to create their own work. Anywhere – on the fringe – forming small companies and producing their own work. Letting people see them at work. 'Nothing will come of nothing', as King Lear said once upon a time.

Anthony Sher

Trained at Webber Douglas Academy. Born in South Africa. Repertory seasons at Liverpool Everyman Theatre, Nottingham Playhouse, Edinburgh Lyceum. In London played in *Teeth 'n' Smiles* and *Cloud Nine* at the Royal Court Theatre. *John, Paul, George, Ringo and Bert*, *Goosepimples*, *Gone West* (National Theatre) *King Lear*, *Tartuffe*, *Mayday*, *Richard III* and *Red Noses* with the Royal Shakespeare Company. Television includes *The History Man* and films *Shadey*. He is also author of the book *Year of the King*.

A.R.   How did you come to be an actor?

A.S.   Well, I was always going to be an artist and it was always assumed that I would leave South Africa and go to somewhere like Italy and study at an art school. I'm not sure how that ambition changed course in Cape Town. I was always terribly shy and I was sent to what were known as elocution lessons – to get me out of myself.

A.R.   Did Shakespeare cross your path early on?

A.S.   Well, not really. I remember the elocution teacher was very keen on the modern plays that were being published then – and I know we worked on Pinter which actually led me to use the part of Mick in *The Caretaker* for my subsequent auditions in England for a place in drama school. But I had very little idea of anything at the time and I didn't do very much acting.

A.R.   When you came to London to audition finally was it your first visit here?

A.S.   Yes, and my parents had booked the audition for the Central School and found me a bed-sit in Swiss Cottage and being completely naive it was assumed that this was where I would be going. Two days later in what was a completely strange country I found myself doing this audition piece and I can remember very clearly sitting in the antechamber afterwards and the registrar popping her head round the door and saying balefully to a group of us sitting there, 'Sorry, none of you'.

A.R.   An immediate rejection.

A.S.   Absolutely shattering. In fact I refused to believe it and went back to check, feeling 'they couldn't mean me'. Luckily we were still in time to get into the RADA auditions, which I did and got a letter from them saying 'not only are you rejected but we strongly advise you to think about another career'. So there I was – a bit stranded, not knowing where to go next. I finally made it into Webber Douglas where I finally realised that this was where I belonged. It seemed to suit me and I seemed to suit it and I felt comfortable.

A.R.   Can you remember anything of that audition?

A.S.   I can remember doing my Mick again from *The Caretaker* and for Shakespeare I did an outrageous choice of Cardinal Wolsey from *Henry VIII*, which I don't think I shall ever be suited to playing.

A.R.   On reflection, what do you feel about drama training?

A.S.   I think it's terribly important for people to train. Acting is not a profession where you can simply stroll on – although I know a lot of fine actors have done that. I learnt an enormous amount and felt then as I do now that there really isn't enough training. Particularly the physical side of the work – where there isn't nearly enough. I think we are under-trained physically here, unlike the Continental or the American actor who are trained as acrobats of gymnasts. In England we concentrate on the voice.

A.R.   Playing *Richard III* combines both of these features for you in a way that makes your point.

A.S.   Yes, it does. Playing Richard is so bound up with physical attitude, and I think that as actors we are not well enough equipped to meet that kind of physical thinking in that kind of role. The Alexander technique would be invaluable if it were properly included in all drama training programmes. And I think you find it goes beyond drama school, in say a company like the RSC, where we have the top person in voice but do not have the equal in physical advice and guidance.

A.R.   What you are saying is that everyone seems to miss the work of Litz Pisk [a legendary movement teacher at Central School] who had such movement sense.

A.S.   I remember when I was working as a dogsbody in the 59 Theatre Company in Manchester a group of Central School students came to be the spirits in a production of *The Tempest* and these were Pisk trained and had, it seemed to me then, a marvellous range of body language. You do see this much more in foreign companies and I think if we in Britain could match the physical and the vocal more we would really be on top with our training resources.

A.R.   Are you saying that this combination of vocal and physical training stems from the demands of the classical play, like *Richard III*, or do you think a different approach is needed for the modern writer?

A.S.   No, I don't think so. The big difference is the dimension of verse, obviously, and you have to live through that differently. Classical acting is really quite a recent thing for me so it's a case of speaking the verse as naturally as possible but observing it's rhythms and structure.

A.R.   How do you feel about young people wanting to become actors, these days?

A.S.   When it comes to acting people will always say 'Don't –
you're going to get hurt', and of course you won't believe
them. And you will get hurt. I think it's a terribly cruel
profession – it's always YOU that is being rejected, the meat
market side of the business. It's hurtful when you see good
actors out of work and the way in which their confidence is
corroded by the system. I think there should be a more
stringent system of entry into the drama schools so that there
is a higher standard of work achieved by the time they come
to join the profession. Auditions are quite unreal – I mean,
how can anyone show what they are about by coming into a
room and doing the opening speech of a play? In playing a
part you have a whole journey of rehearsals behind you.

A.R.   So how would you recommend that actors are cast?

A.S.   In the profession I would much prefer to see work generated
by the directors, and the casting directors taking more trouble
to go round and see the actor at work, taking people on the
basis of work they had already seen. Even the interview
system is not an ideal one – once again you're having to sell
yourself – and if you're a character actor like I am I cannot
show myself without being somebody else. One has very
little to offer in an interview and one sits there feeling rather
embarrassed.

A.R.   That sort of system is not so easy for actors looking for their
first job but easier when you are well known.

A.S.   Well yes, but let me say that I gave up going to auditions well
before I became well known through *The History Man*, on
television. I gave up because I felt insulted. I think you have to
stand by what you believe. I have been lucky, I suppose. One
job *has* led to another but I do remember a particular film
audition which I walked out of, much to the concern of
everyone, my agent, and the casting director. I was thought
to be getting above myself because I refused to sight read a
scene. I offered tapes of myself. But it was useless. No, I do
not believe in the audition system.

A.R.   Well, you're obviously not asked to audition now.

A.S.   It is a privilege; and one doesn't forget that. Working with the
RSC is a pleasure and it's very secure so you can concentrate
on the work in hand. I must confess I find being a complete
freelance is a strain and I love the family feeling of a company.
But some actors prefer the risks. They like to live dangerously.

A.R.   Rather than act dangerously. Would you say that you are building a reputation in eccentric roles?

A.S.   I do see myself as a character actor, it's true. But not necessarily eccentric – that just sounds a gimmick. Finding a character that is true in every moment is quite another matter.

Michael Denison and Dulcie Gray

Met at drama school, married in 1939, honeymooned in weekly rep in Aberdeen and have starred together in more West End productions than any living theatrical partnership. These include *Candida* and *Heartbreak House* by Shaw; *The Wild Duck* by Ibsen; *Where Angels Fear to Tread*, from E.M. Forster; *On Approval* by Frederick Lonsdale and *Bedroom Farce* by Alan Ayckbourn (for the National Theatre).

Michael Denison's best known film role was Algie in *The Importance of Being Earnest* and he appeared with Dulcie in *My Brother Jonathan*. Recently they have both played in a major revival of *The School for Scandal* and have toured the Near and Far East.

Dulcie is the author of twenty-two works – seventeen crime stories, two novels, two plays and a book on the conservation of butterflies. She and Michael have collaborated on a 'young person's guide to the theatre' and Michael has written two volumes of joint memoirs – *Overture* and *Beginners and Double Act*.

A.R.   You both went into the theatre together from the same drama school?

M.D.   That's right – the Webber Douglas Academy. We went into weekly rep in Aberdeen.

D.G.   At first it was only Michael that was going but on hearing that we were hoping to marry they decided to have me as well.

A.R.   And since then you've worked a great deal together?

M.D.   In sixty-four stage productions, so far – starring in twenty-six of them in London. But first, for me everything was interrupted by six years of army service after which like so many others I had to start again. Fortunately for us both, Dulcie had become a star both in theatre and films.

A.R.   When did you start acting?

M.D.   Playing female parts at school – until my voice broke.

D.G.   For me it was also at school playing Sir Andrew Aguecheek. So we both started by playing the opposite sex. But I think I got into drama professionally in the first place by accident. I was told there was an acting scholarship going and I was broke so I took an audition and by a marvellous chance, won the scholarship.

A.R.   Can you remember what you did?

D.G.   Absolute total recall – it was Portia's famous 'The quality of mercy is not strained' from *The Merchant of Venice* – and mercy was what I was asking for, literally, at that moment. Anyway the moment I trod the stage I felt completely at home. I can't explain it more than that.

A.R.   What was the training about in those pre-war days?

M.D.   Much as today, I would think. There was a lot of concentration on the voice and good diction. I came to the school with considerable amateur experience of Shakespeare with the Oxford University Dramatic Society and had even played in a real theatre in Oxford. So the school's first job was to cut me down to normal proportions – which they did. I think the persons who helped me most were the professional actors who were playing in the West End and came to us as teachers during the day.

D.G.   Ellen O'Malley, though she had long retired, was a wonderful teacher too. She was marvellous at getting people to let go of inhibitions I remember. She had played a lot of Shaw including *Candida*; and created Ellie Dunn in *Heartbreak House*, named after her by Shaw.

M.D.   And perhaps even more to us as modern actors was Alison Legatt, then playing with Noël Coward and Gertrude Lawrence every evening.

D.G.   Yes, she was the first person who made me realise that acting was more than just speaking and doing. You had to understand and project what made your character tick.

A.R.   When you work now with young actors do you notice great differences in their approach to acting from your own?

M.D.   Well, the majority have begun on TV rather than weekly rep – resulting in a gain in 'reality' and a loss in audibility. They have also had to face greatly increased competition both to get into drama school and into the profession. When I went to Webber Douglas they practically fell on any man as a rare species. I remember there was seventy-five girls to seven men at the time.

A.R.   So getting a good part in the end of term productions was much more competitive for you, Dulcie?

D.G.   Oh, much; just like the profession itself in a way. I believe the ratio of men's jobs to women's is 8 to 1.

A.R.   Would you say that most of your professional careers have been spent on the stage?

D.G.   Yes. Perhaps the best decade was the sixties when we played a lot of Shaw, Wilde and Ibsen. These included *Candida*, *Heartbreak House*, *The Wild Duck* and *An Ideal Husband* in which we agreed to play the dreadful Chilterns.

A.R.   Why dreadful?

M.D.   As you know, Wilde's full names were Oscar Fingal O'Flaherty Wills Wilde. It was said of *An Ideal Husband* that the characters of Lord Goring, Lord Caversham and Mrs Chevely were the work of Oscar Wilde and Sir Robert and Lady Chiltern of Fingal O'Flaherty.

A.R.   Has the position of the director changed in theatre for you over the years?

M.D.   I think it has changed. Directors are more autocratic and powerful than they were – particularly in casting. More autocratic and more absentee than before. Sometimes they give you the feeling that they have done you a great favour by attending rehearsals and at the end of the rehearsal period it's 'Bye-bye loves, now you do your thing and I'll go off and do another'. Directors should keep their finger on the pulse of a production throughout it's run.

A.R.   Which leads to the usual problems associated with casting and auditioning. Do you think there's a better means of selection, other than what seem generally to be regarded as a rather barbaric system?

M.D.   Of course it's barbaric. But what alternative is there if you are unknown to a potential employer? It's a kind of exam – and it's important to school yourself to be good at exams.

A.R.   One of the biggest questions for young actors today is the problem of becoming members of Equity in order to work in the business for which they have trained. Michael, you have done a lot of work both with and for Equity, what do you feel about the present day students' dilemma?

M.D.   Well, it is a dilemma. I've never entirely agreed with the policy of restricted entry, although one knows all the arguments why this has been necessary. I think we have to remember at all times that we belong to a profession in which there cannot be qualifications. The individual's employment involves a subjective judgement on the part of someone else. I would like to think that the problem of entry into Equity could be resolved in the future – difficult as it is. Perhaps graduates of a number of drama schools might be given a provisional Equity card requiring a minimum number of engagements (and/or weeks) to be worked within the two or three years of it's validity, if the holder is to be accepted into full membership.

A.R.   Is it true that within the membership of Equity there is a fair proportion of deadwood?

M.D.   Well, with a membership of 32,000 and an unemployment level of 70% it follows that there are many members who get little or no work within the profession. It would be harsh, however, to stigmatise them as deadwood. A performer can only prove his talent by performing – meanwhile by their subscriptions members play an important part in making Equity effective.

A.R.   Has the profession become too large?

D.G.   There will always be more people wanting to act than there are jobs available.

M.D.   The acting profession has actually grown smaller since, say, 1900. Provincial cities which had ten to twelve theatres now have one or two and probably there were double the number of actors at that time. Standards were variable, of course, and first the cinema and then television wiped out a lot of bad theatre as well as some good.

A.R.   Do you think the training of young actors should be more orientated towards television?

D.M.   It is the most important medium for getting known by the general public and affecting the attitude of employers but the theatre is still the best place for learning your trade. As Richard Attenborough once said to me, 'If you haven't learnt to play to an audience that is present, how can you expect to play to one that isn't?'

Appendix A

Regional Arts Associations

The following names and addresses will enable you find out about local facilities, and help you to discover more about theatre activity in your own area. Additionally, a list of regional drama advisers is provided, who are the best people to advise on any local companies and the local training facilities available.

There is no doubt that a large number of pre-drama school courses are now run, and these are usually helpful, particularly when you have not had the opportunity to try yourself as an actor before. In fact, the number of such opportunities has proliferated in the last twenty years, and everyone hopes that these services will continue, even in the face of many local authority financial cuts.

All information about getting grants and how they are apportioned and administered are available from these sources, and if you are really intent on gaining professional training in acting, you are going to need all the information you can get before applying to drama school. So do make sure you get yourself organised in this respect.

(NB: Only directorial staff and those officers having particular responsibility for drama and general information services are named here. More information about the aims and policies of the Regional Arts Associations can be found in the *British Theatre Directory*.)

East Midlands Arts Mountfields House, Forest Road, Loughborough LE11 3HU
Tel. (0509) 218292
Director John Buston; **Deputy Director** Mike Hussey; **Senior Officer (Drama and Dance)** Helen Flach
Nottinghamshire, Derbyshire (excluding the High Peak) Leicestershire, Northamptonshire
(They also fund the Buckinghamshire Arts Association)

Eastern Arts Association 8/9 Bridge Street, Cambridge CB2 0UA
Tel. (0223) 357596
Director Jeremy Newton; **Assistant Director (General and Community Arts)** Dick Chamberlain; **Information Officer** Roger Wollen; **Drama Officer** Richard Hogger
Bedfordshire, Cambridgeshire, Essex, Hertfordshire, Norfolk, Suffolk

Greater London Arts 20 Gainsford Street, London SE1 2NE
Tel. (071) 403 9013
Director Pat Abraham
The area of the 32 London Boroughs (which includes Middlesex and parts of Surrey, Kent, Essex and Hertfordshire) and the City of London

Lincolnshire and Humberside Arts St Hugh's, 23 Newport, Lincoln LN1 3DN
Tel. (0522) 33555
Director Clive Fox; **Assistant Director** Chris Buckingham
Lincolnshire and Humberside

Merseyside Arts 3 Bluecoat Chambers, School Lane, Liverpool L1 3BX
Tel. (051) 709 0671
Director Peter Booth; **Assistant Director/Arts** Duncan Fraser; **Arts Development Officer** (Drama and Literature) Theresa Griffin
Metropolitan County of Merseyside, Cheshire districts of Holton, Ellesmere Port, Neston and the West Lancashire District

North Wales Arts Association 10 Wellfield House, Bangor, Gwynedd
Tel. (0248) 353248 (Bangor)   Tel. (0352) 58403 (Mold)
Director D. Llion Williams
Clwyd, Gwynedd and Montgomery area of Powys

North West Arts 12 Harter Street, Manchester M1 6HY
Tel. (061) 228 3062
Director Raphael Gonley; **Deputy Director** Sally Medlyn; **Drama Officer** Ivor Davies
Lancashire, Cheshire, the High Peak of Derbyshire and Greater Manchester

Northern Arts 10 Osborne Terrace, Newcastle upon Tyne NE2 1NZ
Tel. (0632) 816 334
Director Peter Stark; **Drama Officer** Sheila Harborth
Cleveland, Cumbria, County Durham, Northumberland, Tyne and Wear

South East Arts Association 10 Mount Ephraim, Tunbridge Wells, Kent TN4 8AS
Tel. (0892) 41666
Director Christopher Cooper; **Deputy Director** Richard Moore; **Drama Officer** Robert Henry
Kent, Surrey and East Sussex

South East Wales Arts Association Victoria Street, Cwmbran, Gwent NP44 3YT
Tel. (063 33) 67530
Director Hugo Perks; **Deputy Director** Nigel Emery
Counties of Gwent, Mid-Glamorgan and South Glamorgan and districts of Brecknock and Radnor in the county of Powys

South West Arts Breadninch Place, Gandy Street, Exeter, Devon EX4 3LS
Tel. (0392) 218188
Director Martin Rewcastle
Cornwall, Devon, most of Dorset, Gloucestershire, Somerset, County of Avon

Southern Arts Association 19 Southgate Street, Winchester, Hants S023 9DQ
Tel. (0962) 55099
Director Bill Dufton; **Deputy Director** David Altshul; **Theatre Officer** Fiona Ellis; **Information, Marketing and Literature Officer** Keiran Phelan; **Assistant Director/General Arts Officer** Stephen Boyce
Berkshire, Hampshire, Isle of Wight, Oxfordshire, West Sussex, Wiltshire and Bournemouth, Poole and Christchurch districts of Dorset

West Midlands Arts 82 Granville Street, Birmingham B1 2LH
Tel. (021) 631 3121
Director Geoff Sims; **Assistant Director (Arts, Music, Dance)** Dorothy Wilson; **Community Arts Officer** Alison Shotbolt; **Drama Officer** Alan Rivett
West Midlands area, Hereford and Worcester County, Staffordshire, Warwickshire and Shropshire

West Wales Association for the Arts Dark Gate, Carmarthen, Dyfed SA31 1QL
Tel. (0267) 234248
Director Carwyn Roger
Dyfed and West Glamorgan

Yorkshire Arts Association Glyde House, Glydegate, Bradford, Yorkshire BD5 0BQ
Tel. (0274) 723051
Director Roger Lancaster; **Drama Officer** Shea Connolly
South, West and North Yorkshire

Drama Advisers

(taken from the 1990 *British Theatre Directory*)

For all London Boroughs contact the relevant council offices for further information.

ABERDEEN
a) **Graham Biggs**, Drama Adviser
South City and Kincardine Deeside and Moray District
Old Academy, School Hill, Aberdeen AB1 1JT
Tel. (0224) 646612
b) **Laurence Gray**, Drama Adviser
North City, Gordon District and Banff/Buchan Districts
Woodhill House, Ashgrove Road West, Aberdeen AB9 2LA
Tel. (0224) 682222 ext 2698

AVON
Iain Ball, Senior Adviser English and Drama
Avon House North, St James Barton, Horsefair, Bristol
Tel. (0272) 290777 ext 556

BERKSHIRE
Marigold Ashwell, Adviser
The Drama Centre, Beechwood Primary School, Ambleside Close,
Woodley, Reading RG5 4JJ
Tel. (0734) 441513

BIRMINGHAM
Roy Hawksworth, General Inspector (Drama)
Education Department, Margaret Street, Birmingham B3 3BU
Tel. (021) 235 2457

CHESHIRE
Simon Taylor, Senior County Drama Adviser
County Hall, Chester CH3 7DG
Tel. (0244) 602424

CLWYD
Derek Hollins, County Drama Adviser & Director of Theatre Clwyd
Outreach Education Dept., Shire Hall, Mold, Clwyd
Tel. (0352) 2121 ext 572 or 56331 ext 269

DERBYSHIRE
Joan Wilcox, County Adviser for Drama
Education Advisers Office, Derbyshire College of Higher Education,
Chatsworth Hall, Chesterfield Road, Matlock
Tel. (0629) 582 383

DEVON
Terry Jones, County Drama Adviser
Education Department, County Hall, Exeter EX2 4QG
Tel. (0392) 77977
John Percival, Advisory Teacher for Drama (West Devon),
Area Education Office, Civic Centre, Plymouth, Devon
Tel. (0752) 223594

DURHAM
Kevin Graham, County Drama Adviser,
Education Advisers Department, Neville's Cross Centre, Darlington
Road, Durham City DH1 4SY
Tel. (091) 3847325

ESSEX
Roderick Passant, Inspector of Education (with special responsibility
for Drama)
Essex County Council Education Dept., P.O. Box 47, Threadneedle
House, Market Road, Chelmsford
Roger Parsley, Drama Specialist to West Essex,
The Playhouse, Playhouse Square, Harlow, Essex CM20 1LS
Tel. (0279) 418943 (24 hr service).

GLASGOW
Ronnie A. F. Mackie, Staff Tutor in Speech and Drama
Education Office, 129 Bath Street, Glasgow G2 2SY
Tel. (041) 204 2900

GRAMPIAN
Graham Biggs, Drama Adviser,
Education Advisers Centre, Somerhill Academy, Stronsay Drive,
Aberdeen
Tel. (0224) 208205

GWENT
Howard Moore, County Drama Adviser
County Hall, Cwmbran, Gwent
Tel. (063 33) 6771

HAMPSHIRE
Alistair Black, Senior Adviser for Speech and Drama
Education Office, Birch House, Barley Way, Fleet GU13 8YB
Tel. (0252) 812 333

HARROW
David Marigold, Adviser for English and Drama
Education Office, Civic Centre, Harrow HA1 2UW

HERTS
Dennis Hamley and **Richard Andersen**, English and Drama Advisers
Education Offices, County Hall, Hertford
Tel. (0992) 555 555

KENT
David Townsend, Inspector for Drama
North Kent Area, Education Office, Mountbatten House, 28 Military
Road, Chatham ME4 4JE
Tel. (0634) 407300

KNOWSLEY
Paul Morris, Music and Drama Adviser
Education Office, Huyton Hey Road, Huyton, Merseyside
Tel. (051) 480 5111

LANCASHIRE
Frank Bacon, County Adviser (with special responsibility for Speech
and Drama)
P.O. Box 61 County Hall, Preston, PR1 8RJ
Tel. (0772) 54868 ext 3658

LEEDS
David Morton, Inspector of Schools (with special responsibility for
Drama)
Advisory Division, Department of Education, Selectapost 17, Merrion
House, 110 Merrion Centre, Leeds LS2 8DT
Tel. (0532) 463824

LEICESTERSHIRE
Maurice Gilmour, County Drama Adviser
Advisory Centre, County Hall, Glenfield, Leicestershire LE3 8RF
Tel. (0533) 323232

LOTHIAN
John A. Turner, Adviser in Drama
Dean Education Centre, Belford Road, Edinburgh EH4 3DS
Tel. (031) 343 1931

NEWCASTLE
Roger Hancock, Drama Adviser, Pendower Hall, Teachers' Centre,
West Road, Newcastle-upon-Tyne NE15 6PP
Tel. (091) 2743620
Sara Kemp (Drama) Advisory Teacher's Benwell Dance Centre, Fox
and Hounds Lane, Newcastle-upon-Tyne NE15 6LR
Tel. (091) 274 2911

NORTHAMPTONSHIRE
William Shaw, County English and Drama Adviser
Education Offices, Floor 2, Northampton House, Northampton NN1 2HX
Tel. (0604) 236256

NORTHUMBERLAND and NORTH TYNESIDE
Keith J. Williams, Drama Adviser for the County of Northumberland and Metropolitan Borough of North Tyneside
Education Department, County Hall, Morpeth, Northumberland NE61 2EF
Tel. (0670) 514343

NOTTINGHAMSHIRE
Mrs Joan Ellis, Senior Advisory Drama Teacher
Meadowholme, Stubbin Lane, Worksop
Tel. (0909) 472933

OXFORDSHIRE
Geoff Dean, County Drama Adviser
Education Department, Macclesfield House, New Road, Oxford OX1 1NA
Tel. (0865) 810504

POWYS
John Greatorex, County Drama Adviser
Director Theatr Powys, The Drama Centre, Llandrindod Wells, Powys
Tel. (0597) 4444

SHROPSHIRE
Peter Travers, County English Adviser
Education Department, The Shire Hall, Abbey Foregate, Shrewsbury SY2 6ND
Tel. (0743) 254506

SOMERSET
John Coultas, County Inspector for Drama
Education Department, County Hall, The Crescent, Taunton, Somerset
Tel. (0823) 333451 ext 5774
Margaret Bundey, Advisory Teacher for Drama
(address as above).
Peter Hossent, Advisory Teacher for Drama,
The Drama Centre, Peckleford, Yeovil, Somerset
Tel. (0935) 21262
Bernard Coulter
(County Hall as above)

STAFFORDSHIRE
Mrs J. Dutton, Head of Department of Art and Design and Drama,
Chadwick Annex (Burton Technical College), Mill Hill Lane, Winshill,
Burton-on-Trent.
Tel. (0283) 69111

SUFFOLK
Ray Dyer, Drama/English Adviser
Education Dept., Shire Hall, Bury St. Edmunds, Suffolk IP33 2AN
Tel. (0284) 722142

SURREY
Mrs Kay Dudeney, County Drama Inspector
Guildford Education Office, 14a/b North Street, Guildford, Surrey
Tel. (0483) 572881

SUSSEX, EAST
Michael Kremer, Adviser in English and Drama
Education Offices, County Hall, St. Anne's Crescent, Lewes BN7 1SG
Tel. (0273) 481000

SUSSEX, WEST
Anne Fenton, Country Drama Adviser
County Hall, Chichester, W. Sussex PO19 1RF
Tel. (0243) 777792

TRAFFORD
Garth Jones, Drama Adviser
Education Offices, The Town Hall, Sale, Cheshire M33 1ZF
Tel. (061) 872 2101

TYNESIDE, SOUTH
David Griffiths, General Adviser (Drama)
The Town Hall, South Shields, South Tyneside NE33 2RL
Tel. (091) 455 4321 ext 5350

WAKEFIELD
Graham Allan, General Adviser (Drama)
Education Office, 8 Bond Street, Wakefield, Yorks WF1 2QL
Tel. (0924) 290900 ext 5656

WEST GLAMORGAN
Godfrey Evans, County Adviser in Speech and Drama
Advisers' Office, West Glamorgan Education Centre, Oxford Street,
Swansea, West Glamorgan
Tel. (0792) 71111 ext 3374

WIGAN
Ken Gouge, Drama Adviser
Gateway House, Standish Gate, Wigan
Tel. (0942) 827946/7

WILTSHIRE
Roger Day, Drama Adviser
County Hall, Trowbridge, Wiltshire
Tel. (02214) 3641 ext 2492

WOKINGHAM
Marigold Ashwell (Drama Co-ordinator),
Wokingham Teacher's Centre, Wokingham, Surrey
Tel. (0734) 787503

Appendix B

The following appendix lists the major acting courses available at colleges and schools in the UK which are members of the conference of drama schools. Only very brief and basic information has been given, and it's recommended that you refer to the complete prospectus of each institution for full details of courses, conditions of entry and current fees.

Grants

There are few mandatory grants; only the Rose Bruford College, Manchester Polytechnic School of Theatre and Central School of Speech and Drama offer some courses which qualify for mandatory grants. Local Educational Authorities can give discretionary grants to students studying on National Council of Drama Training accredited courses. Not all courses offered by members of the Conference of Drama Schools are accredited by NCDT. Individuals should be consulted about their courses.

Arts Educational Schools
12 Errol Street, London EC1

The following courses are offered:
3 year drama training course
3 year musical theatre course in dance, drama and singing
3 year course in classical ballet and modern dance
1 year acting company refresher course for professionals and post-graduates

Auditions are held at various times of the year for entry after September. Prospective students should prepare two extracts of not more than three minutes duration, one from the works of Shakespeare, or a classical author, and one from a modern playwright.

Students must be 18 or over.

The three years training are structured on the basis of the first year's emphasis on voice and movement. Students begin performing in studio conditions in their second year and build up to a third year of full productions in both the studio and main theatre, concentrating on showcase productions for agents, casting directors, etc. The Golden Lane Theatre seats an audience of 400 and the Burbage Studio about 100.

There is no stage management course, but students are well-grounded in the essentials of preparing a prompt book and the overall running of a production, so they know what is required of the assistant stage manager (ASM), a position which may come their way on completion of the course.

Birmingham School of Speech Training and Dramatic Art
45 Church Road, Edgbaston, Birmingham B15 3SW

The school offers a 3 year course in drama training

Auditions are held prior to each annual intake in September, and comprise selections of not more than two minutes in length from Shakespeare, a modern author, a lyrical poem and a song. Sight reading, improvisation and movement will be set at the time of audition.

Students must be over the age of 18.

So you want to be an actor 72

Five to seven plays are presented each term in the college theatre. Students take part in the design and construction of all sets for all productions and under staff supervision they are responsible for stage management, lighting and the making of costumes and properties. At the end of the second year and during the final year of training a small number of touring productions visit such venues as The Minack Theatre, Cornwall, The Cabin Studio, Stafford and some Midlands schools and colleges. There is closed-circuit television equipment and facilities for radio technique classes in a fully equipped studio.

Bristol Old Vic Theatre School
2 Downside Road, Clifton, Bristol BS8 2XF

The following courses are offered:
2 and 3 year acting courses
1 year post-graduate course
2 year technical and stage management course
1 year stage design course
1 year wordrobe course
1 year advanced diploma in stage design

The 2 year acting course covers the same ground as the 3 year course, but with greater intensity and speed and is therefore better suited to the mature student, the drama or English department post-graduate or those with some theatre experience already to their credit.

Auditions are held in Bristol between early November and late April. After the 'preliminary' auditions candidates may be invited to attend one of a number of weekend schools, which are held in late January and the middle of May. Technical course students are interviewed in Bristol by appointment between January and March.

Up to 6 places on the acting course and 4 on the technical course are open to students from overseas. Auditions for these are held in London and Bristol.

Students are accepted between the ages of 18 and 30.

The school was opened by Laurence Olivier in October 1946, soon after the foundation of the Bristol Old Vic Company itself. It has maintained its aims to train and prepare actors and actresses for a career in acting with a particular emphasis on preparation for work in the classical repertoire. It is completely self-financing.

During the final year of study students appear in public productions at various theatres in Bristol, culminating in a season at the Theatre Royal and New Vic Studios, when agents, managers and casting directors can see the work. There are close links with the BBC, and HTV, which contributes a lot to the television and radio training both for acting students and those on the technical courses.

Central School of Speech and Drama
Embassy Theatre, Eton Avenue, Swiss Cottge, London NW3

The following courses are offered:
3 year acting course
2 year higher national diploma in stage management
4 year B.Ed Hons in drama and spoken language, in conjunction with Thames Polytechnic
1 year full-time advanced diploma course in speech and drama. (For experienced teachers)
4 year B.Sc Hons in speech and language pathology in conjunction with the Polytechnic of Central London
1 year full-time advanced diploma course in voice studies, designed for those with experience in speech and drama teaching, the professional theatre, or speech therapy.
1 year full-time Central school/Sesame joint certificate in the use of drama and movement in therapy.

Auditions for the acting course are held at intervals through the year for the subsequent session and may also be held in the USA in the spring for those unable to travel to London. All American students should apply to the school in the first instance.

Students are admitted between the ages of 17 and 25 for the acting course.

The Central School was founded in 1906 by Elsie Fogarty, and it has occupied the Embassy Theatre, Swiss Cottage and adjacent studios since 1956.

The acting course is 'concerned with the development of the actor's imagination, with the lively and penetrating study of a variety of texts, and with the development of vocal and physical expressiveness and skill'. In the final year students present about 16 public productions, including late-night shows at the Embassy Theatre, the Studio and on tour at the Robin Hood Theatre, Averham.

The stage management course concentrates on lighting and sound techniques and provides a good foundation for those who eventually wish to become directors.

Drama Centre, London
176 Prince of Wales Road, London NW5 3PT

The following courses are offered:
3 year full-time course in acting
2 year full-time course for professional instructors

Auditions and interviews are held throughout the year. For the acting course students are expected to prepare a speech from a classical play and one from any modern play of their own choice. Candidates may also be required to improvise. New students are accepted only at the beginning of the autumn term (in September).

There is an upper age limit of 27.

The prospectus states 'You should try to meet actors and actresses who have trained here and you must talk quite openly with the current students, if and when you come to audition, and their representatives who both sit and vote on the entrance committee. But be warned, this is a very hard school; it is also an impecunious one.'

Over the first two years of training the rehearsal exercises can include plays by authors such as Shakespeare, Racine, Chechov, Gorki and Schnitzler. In the third year (only selected students are retained for the third year) plays are produced in public and aim to stretch the student actor 'far beyond the point that would be expected of him on entering the profession'.

Drama Studio London
Grange Court, 1 Grange Road, London W5 5QN

The following courses are offered:
1 year full-time acting course
1 year full-time directing course

55 places are available on the acting course out of 500 applicants; 8 places are available on the directing course, with 100 applicants per year. The minimum age limit is 21. The acting course is N.C.D.T. accredited and discretionary grants are available from some authorities. Audition requirements for the acting course are; an all day interview consisting of group and individual acting, improvisation exercises and sight reading tests. Requirements for the directing course are: interview and practical exercises and some prepared work which will be asked for when the audition appointment is made.

East 15 Acting School
Hatfields, Rectory Lane, Loughton, Essex

The following courses are offered:
3 year full-time acting course
3 year full-time director's course
1 year post-graduate course
2 year acting course
1 year overseas course
1 year stage management course

Auditions are held at the Corbett Theatre and last a full day. Candidates are expected to present three pieces of their own choice; one modern and two classical. They will also be expected to improvise on given themes. For overseas candidates auditions are held in New York, Perth, Toronto and Vancouver.

The director's course offers opportunities for students to direct in the school after completing a first year as actors. Numbers are limited. There is also a 1 year tutor's course, open to East 15 graduates and professional actors who wish to train as tutors, using East 15 methods. Chosen applicants will be paid Equity minimum rates.

Students need to be 18 years of age and over. There is no upper age limit.

The school was founded by Margaret Bury to develop the creative working methods of Joan Littlewood. The three year acting course is described as a classical training based on acting fundamentals. The work is clearly divided into three separate years, using a wide spectrum of classical writers. In the final term modern plays are presented for one or two weekly runs. There is a possibility of some touring. 'Acting is fun', states the school prospectus, going on to say, 'acting is good for people and all people act and like having fun. Serious study does not require a serious face. Laughter and tears, love and hate are close together'.

Guildford School of Acting
20 Buryfields, Guildford, Surrey GU2 5AZ

The following courses are offered:
Performance – acting and musical option
1 year post-graduate course (acting and stage management)
2 year stage management course

Auditions are held at various times between September and June each year. A full day is taken. Details of the audition selections required are available on application. For the acting course a classical piece and a contrasting modern play may be expected.

The school welcomes applications from overseas students, and those unable to attend auditions in England may use sound and video tapes. Auditions are held in the USA in New York at the International Institute of International Education each April following direct applications to Guildford.

The minimum age of entry is 17.

Although there is a distinction between the acting and the musical theatre courses, all students will finally work together in the stage productions that are presented at the end of the training. The point is made in the prospectus that people who want to break into the profession need to be able to act, sing and dance.

The school presents an average of 15 productions every year in their own playhouse. Students sometimes perform at the Bellerby Theatre and from time to time at the Yvonne Arnaud Theatre's Studio theatre. There is also the possibility of some touring. Video projects are undertaken with professional television directors, as well as radio productions.

Guildhall School of Music and Drama
Barbican, London EC2Y 8DT

The following courses are offered:
9 term professional acting course
6 term stage management course

6 term prop making course
3 term scene painting course

Auditions for the acting course are held after October (it is advised that all applications be submitted early in October) and there will be further auditions for short-listed candidates in January or February. Interviews for the stage management course will be held in March; for the scene painting course in May.

The first two terms of the acting course include voice and movement work, work in tumbling, period dance and the Alexander technique, to free the voice and body. The middle terms concentrate on the performing skills, including working for television and radio – the film work being done in association with the National Film School. In the final terms the system changes to that of a repertory company, with professional directors imported (including some from the RSC). Major classical and modern productions are mounted, including musicals.

In the technical training, specialised areas include sound and lighting design and production management (a much overlooked feature of theatre training).

LAMDA (London Academy of Music and Drama)
Tower House, 226 Cromwell Road, London SW5 0SR

The following courses are offered:
3 year acting course
1 year acting course for overseas students (3 terms)
2 year stage management technical theatre course

Auditions are held regularly for an annual intake in September. A selection from classical and modern theatre is required.

Age limit is 18 to 26 for all courses.

'LAMDA is an independent drama school, dedicated to training actors, and stage managers to meet the demands and opportunites of the contemporary professional theatre, and equip them with a strong technical basis for their craft.' This is a simple policy statement given in the prospectus.

The one year course for overseas students on acting concentrates on an approach to Shakespeare and the classics; students may be chosen who already have a professional theatre background in their own country, and the course is popular with students from Canada and the USA.

The flexible stage of the MacOwen Theatre allows for presentation of final productions in many forms: proscenium, in-the-round, open stage or arena staging.

Manchester Polytechnic School of Theatre
The Capitol Building, School Lane, Didsbury, Manchester M20 10HT

A 3 year acting course is offered.

Minimum age of entry is 18, and the annual intake from auditions is approximately 24 students.

The practical content of the course includes work in film and television techniques, carried out with the Polytechnic's School of Film and Television. Technical facilities include a large flexible theatre space, supported by workshop and tutorial space. There is a well-stocked library. Good liaison with Granada and BBC television, and with Radio Manchester.

Communication and imagination are the watchwords of the training here; the prospectus states that 'students are expected to cultivate as wide a view of the theatre as possible and to be prepared to take part in innovations whenever they arise'.

Mountview Theatre School
104 Crouch Hill, London N8

The following courses are offered:
3 year acting course
1 year post-graduate course in acting
2 year stage management course
Part-time courses run in acting for teenagers and children.

Auditions are held regularly in London and abroad. Selection of audition material should be two contrasting pieces, classical and modern. Additionally, candidates may be asked to read at sight, to improvise on any subject, or to sing. The finals audition panel includes guest professionals and the school's principal. There is a limited scholarship fund.

There are two working theatres at the school, an experimental studio, and a proscenium stage. There is a strong emphasis on touring both at home and abroad. Additional private tuition available, which includes coaching for professional auditions for finals students.

Queen Margaret College, Edinburgh
36 Clerwood Terrace, Edinburgh EH12 8TS

A 3 year diploma in drama is offered

Auditions and interviews are held as soon as possible after application from suitable candidates; preference given to candidates whose application reaches the college by 15 December of year before proposed year of entry.

Minimum age of entry is 17.

The first two years are foundation years, with students concentrating on the basic skills of performing and theatre arts. In the third year students select an option for fuller development, either in acting or stage management. The school has been open since 1972, and welcomes students from overseas.

There is strong emphasis on the preparation of students for professional participation in drama as a social art form.

Rose Bruford College
Lamorbey Park, Sidcup, Kent DA15 9DF

The following courses are offered:
3 year theatre arts course (CNAA) qualifying for an honours degree
3 year community theatre arts course
2 year technical theatre arts course

Auditions are held regularly throughout the year.

The minimum age is 18 by the 1st October in the year of entry.

The closest possible links are maintained with working professionals to ensure that what is being taught is relevant to comtemporary needs. Tours are mounted and full-scale productions are put on in London to provide students with a variety of audience experience. The diploma in community theatre devises programmes for children in schools, old people and groups with special needs. The technical course includes stage management, costume and wardrobe technique, lighting, sound and scenery construction.

Royal Academy of Dramatic Art
62–64 Gower Street, London WC1E 6EW

The following courses are offered:
7 term full-time acting course
5 term full-time stage management course

4 term stage electronics course
4 term scene painting and design diploma course
4 term stage carpentry diploma course

Audition sessions usually take place in the spring and winter months, and entry is divided between summer (in 'even' years) and spring and autumn (in 'odd' years). Candidates are expected to perform two pieces of their own choice no longer than 3 minutes each. A classical selection must include a monologue by Shakespeare, Marlowe, Webster,

Tourneur or Ford. (There is a list of certain Shakespeare selections which must be avoided, which will be provided for those who register for entry.) A second piece must be a clear contrast. A number of candidates will be recalled and will also be interviewed by the Principal and Administrator/Registrar.

Auditions for overseas candidates from the USA are held in New York at the Institute of International Education, during the months of December and April.

Students for the acting course should be aged 18 (occasionally a younger student may be admitted). Minimum age of applicants for the stage management course is 17; for specialist courses, 19.

The Academy may award a limited number of scholarships; the amounts endowed are not fixed but the most valuable provides full fee remission. There are twelve scholarships in all, and also two scholarships for American students which are privately endowed; these may provide whole or partial fee remission, according to circumstances.

The Academy was founded by Sir Herbert Beerbohm Tree in 1904 and has provided a comprehensive training for the professional theatre ever since. There are two fully equipped theatres and studio theatre space.

Royal Scottish Academy of Music and Drama
100 Renfrew Street, Glasgow G2 3DB

The following courses are offered:
3 year full-time course leading to BA in dramatic studies, offered through the University of Glasgow
1 year full-time technical course
3 year full-time stage course, leading to a diploma in dramatic art.

Auditions/examinations are held between January and June of each year. Two contrasting audition pieces are required of your own choice, of not less than one minute in length each. All candidates remain for further audition through group improvisation exercises.

The minimum age for entry to both diploma and technical courses is 18.

Originally founded as the Glasgow College of Drama by James Bridie, the Academy has widened its activities considerably and now occupies a new purpose-built conservatoire, with two theatres, TV and radio studios, extensive workshops and all training facilities. The Academy is not confined to Scottish students only.

First year studios and workshops are observed by a public audience, unusual in dramatic training. Television productions and repertory style productions follow, as well as major productions attended by agents, casting directors, etc. The technical course provides training in all aspects of stage management and television technical management, including vision mixing and floor management.

Webber Douglas Academy of Dramatic Art
30 Clareville Street, London SW7 5AP

The following courses are offered:
3 year acting course
2 year acting course
1 year post-graduate course

Auditions are held for all courses between mid-October and May, excluding the months of December and April. Candidates are required to present two contrasting pieces (one Shakespeare, the other modern) each choice not exceeding three minutes in length. It is suggested that one piece should be from a comedy, and that some movement should be included. New York auditions for September entry are held in April at the Institute of International Education, but all applications should be sent to the Academy in London prior to the closing date (20th February).

The 3 year diploma course in acting is not recommended for overseas students and the minimum age is 18. The 2 year diploma course has an age minimum of 20 and is aimed at maturer students who have achieved certain educational standards. Oveseas students should have reached an educational standard sufficient for university entrance in their own country. The 1 year post-graduate course (minimum age of entry 21) is open to UK and overseas applicants who have a university degree and considerable acting experience is also needed.

Scholarships, which are extremely limited, are only available to diploma students in the second and third years, and to post-graduate students for the optional second year.

The Academy was founded as a singing school in 1926, and still maintains a strong emphasis on singing as well as acting. The prospectus states 'Acting is an arduous and exacting profession and, apart from talent, a student must have good health and stamina and be able to work with self-discipline.' The theatre work is presented in the main theatre and at a studio theatre. According to the size of finals groups, 3 to 5 productions are given at the end of the final term. There is concentrated work on television and radio performance.

Welsh College of Music and Drama
Castle Grounds, Cathays Park, Cardiff CF1 3ER

The following full-time courses are offered:
4 year B.Ed (Hons) course, run jointly with South Glamorgan Institute
of Higher Education, for intending teachers of drama
3 year graduate diploma course in drama, leading to University of
Wales diploma
3 year course in drama for performers
1 year post-graduate course in drama for performers
1 year course options, acting or design and stage management

Auditions for the performers courses are held usually in December
and spring for a September entry. Two contrasting pieces are required
(Shakespeare and a modern author) of the candidates own choosing.
Further to this, candidates are selected for a second audition on the
same day with the course tutor and this will involve some movement
and improvisation. Candidates will also be asked to sing unaccompanied.

All courses stipulate a minimum age of 18, and certain educational
qualifications.

In recent years the emergence of new theatre in Wales and the growth of
Welsh television and radio have resulted in a demand for trained
personnel of high calibre. The drama department aims to meet these
demands, as well as preparing students for theatre in the UK.

The following schools offer training but are not members of the
Conference of Drama Schools.

Hertfordshire Theatre School
70 Old Park Road, Hitchin, Herts SG5 2JT

The following courses are offered:
3 year acting and musical theatre course
1 year advanced course for post-graduates and teachers
Apply to the Registrar for a prospectus

The London Academy of Performing Arts
861–863 Fulham Road, London SW6 5HT

The following courses are offered:
2 year acting course

1 year post-graduate course
4 week intensive Summer Shakespeare Acting Course (for students seeking an insight into the classical acting tradition)

The minimum age for entry for the 2 year acting course is 18 and for the post-graduate course it is 20. They are open to UK and overseas students. Auditions are held throughout the year. Applicants should send their application form with a passport-size photograph.

The prospectus says, 'It is the policy of the London Academy of Performing Arts to concentrate on the basic studies of voice and movement, to develop the individual resources of each student, to stimulate the imagination and to free the creative instincts. The aim is to lay the foundations for a secure and firm technique for the actor's future role in the theatre'.

London and International School of Acting (LISA)
138 Westbourne Grove, London W11 2RR

The following courses are offered in a structure that operates a four term year, each term consisting of ten weeks separated by three-week vacations:

1 year post-graduate course
2 year diploma course
3rd year career launching course (post-diploma course)

The post-graduate course is for mature students or those of considerable experience. The minimum age of entry is 18 for the diploma course. On completion of the 2 year diploma course a third year is designed to combine further training, professional opportunities, and a personal management service to further the actor's career opportunities.

The prospectus states 'The school aims to provide a structured training to suit the modern young actor and actress and prepare them thoroughly for a professional career. The courses employ improvisation, observation, sight-reading, script analysis, voice and speech training, dance and 'Actor's Kata', a technique to develop the total capabilities of the body. In laying the emphasis on the Art of Performance, the school's assignment is to develop professionally orientated acting students. Full-time courses commence in October.'

London Theatre School
Memorial Hall, Chapel Yard, 121B Wandsworth High Street, Wandsworth, London SW18 4HZ

The following courses are offered:
2 year full-time acting course
1 year full-time acting course
1 year foundation course
6 month classical acting course

The 2 year course is for students aged 18 and over, the 1 year course is for postgraduate and mature students, the foundation course is for 16–18 year olds and the intensive course is for UK and overseas students.

The prospectus states 'The aim of the school is to offer you the best possible preparation for a successful career in the professional theatre and to equip you for the increasingly varied demands of that career. We place particular emphasis on the study and performance of the works of Shakespeare and the major classical dramatists. We want to teach you the skills you will need for the particular area of theatre in which you want to work. We also want to encourage and develop your individual qualities so that you can progress with confidence, energy and creativity within a structured framework.

The Northern School
Pack Horse Lane, Burslem, Stoke-on-Trent, Staffordshire ST6 4BA

The following courses are offered:
1 year acting course
2 and 3 year acting courses
2 year stage management course
1 and 2 year directing course
1 and 2 year design course

The Oxford School of Drama
Sansomes Farm Studios, Woodstock, Oxford OX7 1ER

The following courses are offered:
1 year post-graduate course
2 year diploma course
summer courses

The Poor School
242–244 Pentonville Road, London N1 9UP

The following course is offered:
six term, 2 year training

This course is run in the evenings and at weekends. In the final two terms some daytime work is involved. There are no age limits, generally students are aged between 18 and 30, but 'no-one should be discouraged from applying solely because of age'. Classes, which are inter-related with the other, include voice and speech, movement, animal study, verse and text study, rehearsal and internal performance, and rehearsal and public performance. An 'agent's evening' is held to present the students at their best and introduce them to the profession.

Appendix C   Summer Schools

The short four to five week summer school is held at the following academies, and applications should be made at least by April for the course running from July to mid-August.

RADA
A three to four week drama workshop is held in August, leading to a certificate. Details are sent out in February to anyone requesting them, applications are considered and a limited number of places are awarded on the basis of information submitted. The course is planned not only for professionals and others with experience, but for those interested in acting, whether or not they intend to make a career in drama.

Webber Douglas Academy
The five week course is suitable for any student seeking an introduction to full-time drama training. The course runs from mid-July to mid-August, and the minimum age is 17. Students may request their work to be assessed and taken into account for their application for entry the following year. A free audition for the main drama training course may also be possible.

LAMDA
A four week course run in July and August which concentrates on Shakespeare, and is open for application in the early part of the year.

GUILDFORD SCHOOL OF ACTING
A three to four week summer school is held each year in July and August. The course is open to anyone over the age of 17 years. There are no educational requirements.

Index